CLASSIC SERMONS ON THE FRUIT OF THE SPIRIT

Kregel Classic Sermon Series

Classic Sermons on Angels
Classic Sermons on the Apostle Paul
Classic Sermons on the Apostle Peter
Classic Sermons on the Attributes of God
Classic Sermons on the Birth of Christ
Classic Sermons on Christian Service
Classic Sermons on the Church
Classic Sermons on the Cross of Christ
Classic Sermons on Death and Dying
Classic Sermons on Faith and Doubt
Classic Sermons on Family and Home
Classic Sermons on the Fruit of the Spirit
Classic Sermons on the Grace of God
Classic Sermons on Heaven and Hell
Classic Sermons on the Holy Spirit
Classic Sermons on Hope
Classic Sermons on Jesus the Shepherd
Classic Sermons on Judas Iscariot
Classic Sermons on Lesser-Known Bible Characters
Classic Sermons on the Lord's Prayer
Classic Sermons on the Love of God
Classic Sermons on the Miracles of Jesus
Classic Sermons on the Names of God
Classic Sermons on the Old Testament Prophets
Classic Sermons on Overcoming Fear
Classic Sermons on the Parables of Jesus
Classic Sermons on Praise
Classic Sermons on Prayer
Classic Sermons on the Prodigal Son
Classic Sermons on the Resurrection of Christ
Classic Sermons on Revival and Spiritual Renewal
Classic Sermons on the Seasons of Life
Classic Sermons on the Second Coming and Other Prophetic Themes
Classic Sermons on the Sovereignty of God
Classic Sermons on Spiritual Warfare
Classic Sermons on Stewardship
Classic Sermons on Suffering
Classic Sermons on the Will of God
Classic Sermons on the Word of God
Classic Sermons on World Evangelism
Classic Sermons on Worship

CLASSIC SERMONS ON THE FRUIT OF THE SPIRIT

Compiled by
Warren W. Wiersbe

Classic Sermons on the Fruit of the Spirit
Compiled by Warren W. Wiersbe

Published by Kregel Publications, a division of Kregel, Inc., P.O. Box 2607, Grand Rapids, MI 49501. Kregel Publications provides trusted, biblical publications for Christian growth and service. Your comments and suggestions are valued.

For more information about Kregel Publications, visit our web site at: www.kregel.com.

Cover photo: PhotoDisc

ISBN 0-8254-4106-4

Printed in the United States of America
1 2 3 4 5 / 06 05 04 03 02

Contents

List of Scripture Texts

Preface

THE *Kregel Classic Sermons Series* is an attempt to assemble and publish meaningful sermons from master preachers about significant themes.

These are *sermons,* not essays or chapters taken from books about themes. Not all of these sermons could be called great, but all of them are *meaningful.* They apply the truths of the Bible to the needs of the human heart, which is something that all effective preaching must do.

While some are better known than others, all of the preachers whose sermons I have selected had important ministries and were highly respected in their day. The fact that a sermon is included in this volume does not mean that either the compiler or the publisher agrees with or endorses everything that the man did, preached, or wrote. The sermon is here because it has a valued contribution to make.

These are sermons about *significant* themes. The pulpit is no place to play with trivia. The preacher has thirty minutes in which to help mend broken hearts, change defeated lives, and save lost souls; he can never accomplish this demanding ministry by distributing homiletical tidbits. In these difficult days we do not need clever pulpiteers who discuss the times; we need dedicated ambassadors who will preach the eternities.

The reading of these sermons can enrich your spiritual life. The studying of them can enrich your skills as an interpreter and expounder of God's truth. However God uses these sermons in your life and ministry, my prayer is that His church around the world will be encouraged and strengthened by them.

—WARREN W. WIERSBE

The Fruit of the Spirit

George Campbell Morgan (1863–1945) was the son of a British Baptist preacher and preached his first sermon when he was thirteen years old. He had no formal training for the ministry, but his tireless devotion to the study of the Bible helped him to become one of the leading Bible teachers of his day. Rejected by the Methodists, he was ordained into the Congregational ministry. He was associated with Dwight L. Moody in the Northfield Bible conferences and as an itinerant Bible teacher. He is best known as the pastor of the Westminster Chapel, London (1904–1917 and 1933–1943). During his second term, Dr. D. Martyn Lloyd-Jones was his associate.

Morgan published more than sixty books and booklets, and his sermons are found in *The Westminster Pulpit* (London: Hodder and Stoughton, 1906–1916). This sermon was taken from *The Westminster Pulpit,* volume 1.

1

The Fruit of the Spirit

The fruit of the Spirit is love, joy, peace, longsuffering, kindness, goodness, faithfulness, meekness, temperance: against such there is no law. (Galatians 5:22–23)

"The fruit of the Spirit is love." While perhaps the sublimest statement the Bible contains concerning God is the brief monosyllabic declaration of the apostle of love, "God is love," I am inclined to think this is the sublimest statement it makes concerning the issue and finality of Christianity.

It is quite impossible to exhaust so broad and spacious a statement in one meditation. If we take the widest outlook, that of the purpose of God in the race, Christianity will have won its victory finally and perfectly when love becomes the sole law of life and conduct. It is certainly true in the narrower realm of the church, in which is deposited and through which is communicated the dynamic that moves toward the larger realization, that in proportion as Christ's church lives in love it is able to fulfill its mission in the world. Again, Christianity wins its final victory in the individual life when that life becomes love-mastered, love-driven. That is the first meaning of the text, although I have set it last in order.

The apostle here has been describing the difference between

the works of the flesh and the fruit of the Spirit. He gathers up the whole truth into this one brief sentence, which he afterward explains by the other words that lie within the compass of my text. Everything is written when this is written, "The fruit of the Spirit is love."

Let us examine this statement in three ways, passing very rapidly over the first two and giving the greater part of our time to the last.

The Method of Christianity in Its Use of the Word *Fruit*

The declaration is, first of all, a revelation of the method of Christianity in its use of the word *fruit.* "The *fruit* of the Spirit is love." It is, in the second place, a revelation of the dynamic of Christianity in the use of the word *Spirit.* "The fruit of the *Spirit* is love." And, finally, it is a revelation of the issue of Christianity in its use of the word *love.* "The fruit of the Spirit is *love.*"

Our thoughts gather around the three outstanding words, "fruit . . . Spirit . . . love," the first indicating the method, the second revealing the power, and the last declaring the issue.

"The fruit of the Spirit is love." The word *fruit* presupposes life. There can be no fruit apart from life. The word *fruit* indicates cultivation. Fruit comes to perfection only in answer to the touch of cultivation. Fruit, finally, suggests sustenance. Fruit is a food. In these simplest thoughts concerning the word we have a revelation of the whole method of Christianity.

Fruit suggests life. The apostle writes, "the *works* of the flesh," but "the *fruit* of the Spirit." As my friend, Samuel Chadwick of Leeds, once forcefully put it, "The word *works* suggests the factory: the word *fruit* suggests the garden."

Works, the works of men, are always operations in the realm of death, and they forevermore contain within themselves the elements of disintegration. Fruit is always an operation in the realm of life, containing within itself the power of propagation.

The finest works that man has ever wrought are all operations in the realm of death. If your quickly moving mind questions me about the flowers and tells me that they are man's work, I reply that it is where man's work ceases and God's begins that life proceeds. Man's work is always an operation in the realm of death. Take the building in which we are gathered. It is useful, necessary, proper, but it could not be erected save as man handled dead materials. The tree in the forest with its rising sap and its budding life was no use to the builder. It must die before man could begin his work. Man's works being operations in the realm of death, they contain within themselves the elements of breakup. While this building was being erected, long before the builder put on the final stone with rejoicing, old mother nature with mossy fingers had begun to pull it down, and, notwithstanding the fact that we have reconstructed it, she is busy destroying it at this moment. As quickly as man works, his work crumbles and passes. That is the figure the apostle used when he was speaking of the flesh. The works of the flesh are operations in the realm of death. The finest thing a man can do within his own self-centered life is a thing of decay and breakup, which perishes and passes and cannot abide.

Fruit is an operation in the realm of life, that mystic fact, which we all know by observation and none of us knows by final analysis and explanation. Life is of God as much in the flowering of a daisy as in the blossoming of stars. It owes its origin to God as surely in the sparrow as in the seraph. Fruit is God's work. You may paint fruit, but it fades upon your canvas though you mix your colors with the skill of a Turner. You may make your fruit of wax, but it perishes, notwithstanding the fact that you put it under a glass case.

Fruit has in it the properties of perpetual life: "the tree bearing fruit, wherein is the seed thereof, after its kind." There is the potentiality in all fruit of unceasing propagation. It is a thing of life. Christianity is a thing of life. The love that is its final fruitage cannot be manufactured; it must grow, and it must grow out of the principle of life.

Fruit implies cultivation. There can be no perfection of fruit without cultivation. Let the tree in your garden run wild, never use the pruning knife, and all the fine quality of the fruit will pass away from it. The fruit of Christianity, which is love, comes to perfection only by the processes of cultivation, not your cultivation, but Jesus'. "I am the true vine, and my Father is the husbandman. . . . ye are the branches" (John 15:1, 5).

Let me turn aside for one brief, passing message to some heart in trouble. You are passing through the fire; you are overwhelmed with sorrow. You crept up to the assembly of the saints feeling inclined to say, "Has God forgotten me? Why this pruning, this beating, this buffeting?" Hear this: The perfection of Christian character comes only by cultivation. "My Father is the husbandman." He holds in His hand the pruning knife. "All chastening seemeth for the present to be not joyous, but grievous: yet afterward . . ." (Heb. 12:11 ASV). God help you to look to the afterward, and to know this, "whom the Lord loveth he chasteneth" (v. 6), and to see that by these processes of cultivation He is perfecting the fruit.

Finally, fruit suggests not merely life and cultivation, it suggests sustenance–sustenance for God. "God is love." God's heart hungers after love. God can be satisfied only with love. Listen to the wailing minor threnody of the old Hebrew prophets. They are from beginning to end the sighing of God after the love of His people. I shall never forget what a revelation of God came into my own life when a few years ago I gave myself to the study of their writings. I had thought of them as men of thunder and found them to be men of tears. I had thought of them as men of wrath, uttering denunciation of sin and proclaiming the terrible judgment of God's holiness. They are all that; but I found that at the back of all the thunder was the infinite disappointment of God because men did not love Him. "How shall I give thee up, Ephraim?" (Hos. 11:8). That is the cry of a Being hungry for love. If you go a little further back in your Bible to the old story in Genesis, you find God saying to Adam, "Where art thou?" (Gen. 3:9). That is not the arresting voice of a policeman. It is the wailing voice of the Father who has lost His child. God is hungry for love. Take a figure nearer home. We believe He is here in this house. He has come to His garden. He is among the branches of His own vine. What is He seeking? Love. The proportion in which He finds love in your heart, dominating, flourishing, mastering, is the proportion in which God is satisfied with you. The fruit of the Spirit that is for the sustenance of God's own heart in its hunger is love.

The Dynamic of Christianity in the Use of the Word *Spirit*

Pass to the second of these thoughts, and I dismiss this even more rapidly. Our text is a revelation of the dynamic of Christianity in the use of the word *Spirit.* Let me only take the thought that Christianity is a life. How is life generated in man? By his being born of the Spirit. If that life needs cultivation toward perfection, how is it cultivated? By the ministry of that Spirit who is grieved when we violate the law of love. If Christianity is indeed the fruit that is sustenance for the very hunger of God's heart, how does it come to its perfect fruitage? Only as my spirit becomes by close identity the very Spirit of Jesus Christ. "If any man hath not the Spirit of Christ, he is none of his" (Rom. 8:9). But if he have the Spirit of Christ, it is the Spirit of love, and God finds the answer to His hunger in me as He finds Christ formed in me by the ministry of the Holy Spirit. The fruit comes through the life that the Spirit gives. The fruit is cultivated toward perfection by the Spirit in all His tender, gracious work in the heart. Love is sustenance for God's hunger, and it is His Holy Spirit in perfect cooperation that makes my spirit Christ's Spirit, and the fruit for which God seeks.

The Issue of Christianity in Its Use of the Word *Love*

Now we come to that which is the plain meaning of the text. "The fruit of the Spirit is love." I can well understand that some of you are saying, "Why do you take this one word *love?*" Because when this one word is uttered there is no more to say. It is perfectly correct to take all the words that follow. The apostle wrote them under inspiration and with deep significance. You will see at once there is difficulty in the text. It reads, "The fruit of the Spirit *is* love, joy, peace, longsuffering, kindness, goodness, faithfulness, meekness, temperance." You feel there is difficulty in saying, "The fruit of the Spirit *is,*" and then reciting nine words. Men have recognized the grammatical difficulty of the "is," and quote the passage, "The fruits of the Spirit are . . ."

That is grammatical. That reads smoothly. Hence the popular supposition that there are nine fruits of the Spirit.

But we have no right to interfere with the text in that way. Our business is to find out what the text really means. The apostle wrote, "The fruit of the Spirit *is* love. . . ." It is one, not nine! It may be objected that the affirmation does not remove the difficulty in the text. The one thing in your Bible that is not inspired is the punctuation. If I were writing this text out for myself I would feel I was perfectly warranted in changing the punctuation, and I would read it like this: "The fruit of the Spirit is love," and then I should indicate a pause by some means other than a comma, say a semicolon and a dash, and then read on: "joy, peace, longsuffering, gentleness, goodness, faith, meekness, temperance." The apostle reaches his climax, and he writes the full and final fact concerning Christian experience in the words, "The fruit of the Spirit is love." Then there breaks upon his consciousness the meaning of love, and in order that we may not treat the word as a small word, that we may not pass it over and imagine there is nothing very much in it, that it is merely a sentimental word, he gives us the qualities and quantities and flavors of the fruit by breaking it up into its component parts. To change the figure, the apostle writes the word *love,* and there surges through his soul all the harmonies of the Christian life. It is a great orchestra–*love*–and he listens and picks out one by one the different qualities of the music: "joy, peace, longsuffering, gentleness, goodness, faith, meekness, temperance."

If you have love, you have all these things. If you lack love, you lack them all. If that can be proved, then I think it is proved that love is the all-inclusive word, and the words that follow break it up and explain its meaning.

Joy. This is a commonplace word. It does not signify an ecstasy that occurs once, and passing leaves the soul on a deader level than it occupied before it came. It does not indicate one of those red days in one's life aflame with high passion. These are not to be undervalued; but this word does not indicate any such experience. *Joy* is a simple word that means cheerfulness, gladness, common delight, that peculiar and wonderful quality which, present in the life, transmutes everything into light and peace and happiness; that consciousness in the life which sings through all the livelong day; that happy cheerfulness, alas! too sadly absent from our life today, which sings in the midst of a November fog just as much as on a glorious June day. What is equal to keeping a man cheerful in all circumstances? Nothing other than love. I make no apology for taking my illustration from that wonderful realm—the newborn love of youth and maiden, of Christ and the church, of the bridegroom and the bride. It is God's own illustration. I read in the old prophets, "I will betroth thee unto me for ever" (Hos. 2:19). Let such love take possession of the heart of youth and maiden, and they are perpetually cheerful. You button your coat around you and say, "It is a drab day." They say, "No, it is saffron." If you say the sky is gray they say it is purple. They are cheerful from morning to night with the cheerfulness that comes with love's first young dream. If you would be cheerful through all vicissitudes of life you must have love in your heart. Love is a singer that never tires. Love is a nightingale that sings while the sun flames and keeps singing when the rains descend. *Joy is love's consciousness.*

Peace. This word indicates not stagnation, but the peace that follows battle—the harmony of opposing forces. What is equal to making peace after battle? Nothing other than love. Two nations are at war. The stronger defeats the other by force, and I take up my newspaper and read that peace has been declared. Is it peace? For all national and political purposes, yes; but in the deepest fact of things it is not peace. If–and it is a great if–the stronger nation can so deal with the conquered nation as to make that conquered nation feel that the conqueror loves it, then you will have peace. Two people are at strife in the church. Forgive the illustration, but these things do exist. They come to me as their pastor and say, "We have settled this business." "How have you settled it?" I ask. "We have agreed that it cannot be settled, so we have decided to bury it and never talk of it again." Then, in God's name, dig it up. That is not peace. The buried hatchet can always be unearthed. Learn to love, and you will have peace. *Peace is love's confidence.*

Longsuffering. May I put that in another form and say *long-temperedness.* I very seldom find people who easily understand that word. Let me suggest another, *short-temperedness.* I find most people understand that. Long-temperedness is the exact opposite of short-temperedness. Long-temperedness is the great and marvelous quality that endures. You heard the great love poem from the Corinthian letter, "Love suffereth long" (1 Cor. 13:4). That is the same word. Love is long-tempered. That is not all Paul said. "Love suffereth long, *and is kind"* (v. 4). That is the marvel of it. You have suffered long, the sense of your own dignity has made you silent; but there comes a day when you say, "I have suffered this long enough, and now . . ." We all know what you mean. That is not love. "Love suffereth long, *and is kind."* Love is the overplus of patience.

Can you think of anything else that would make you longsuffering? I suppose you will agree with me that the most longsuffering people in the world are mothers. Why? I can give you the answer in a word. Because they love. There are all sorts of foolish proverbs abroad. Men tell me that love is blind. Nothing of the kind. Love sees most keenly and acutely and correctly. You tell me I am wrong, and say, "Look at that woman. Her son is going wrong. We have seen it for a long time. She is blind. She does not see it." Let me tell you she saw it long before you did. Then you say, "Why does she not heed us when we try to tell her?" Because "[love] . . . beareth all things, believeth all things, hopeth all things, endureth all things" (v. 7). That is the story of a mother's love. That is long-temperedness. *Long-temperedness is love's habit.*

Kindness. The Greek word here is one which refers not to sentiment, but to service. Kindness is usefulness in a good sense, and always in small things. The word "kindness" refers to that attitude of life which makes men see the little thing that, being done, will minister to some other soul. I submit to you, is there anything equal to maintaining you in the kindness of doing little things except love? I am afraid it must be granted that there may be motives for great philanthropies other than that of love. Amos was a wonderful prophet, and he, when he was dealing with the men of his day, said, "[They] proclaim freewill-offerings and publish them" (Amos 4:5 ASV). Love is not necessarily behind the published gift. It is told of Sir Moses Montefiore that after he had passed away there was found a little book in which were entered gifts that far surpassed those which had been publicly acknowledged during his lifetime. On the front page of this book these words were written, "The gifts which men acknowledge do not count in the ledgers of heaven." That was Hebrew, but it was coming very near to the heart of Christianity. Here is a young man who, if he were talking to me, would tell me he loves his mother. He would even tell me that he was willing to die for her. Nonsense! Stay at home tomorrow night and read to her for half an hour. Kindness is the willingness to do simple things to help other people. When Jesus approaches a subject He says the last thing. According to Him, the cup of cold water, which costs nothing but the trouble of seeing that it is wanted and the giving, counts in heaven. What will make a man keen-eyed enough to see the thousand and one little needs of life and meet them? Nothing but love. *Kindness is love's activity.*

Goodness. Goodness is–just goodness. I wish we used that word more than we do. We have been talking much about holiness–not too much–but we have been talking a great deal too little about righteousness. What is holiness? Rectitude of character. What is righteousness? Rectitude of conduct. What is goodness? Both. *Goodness* is the greatest of all the words. That is one reason why I love the hymn:

> There is a green hill far away,
> Outside a city wall,
> Where the dear Lord was crucified,
> Who died to save us all.
>
> He died that we might be forgiven,
> He died to make us *good,*
> That we might go at last to heaven,
> Saved by His precious blood.
>
> There was no other *good* enough
> To pay the price of sin;
> He only could unlock the gate
> Of heaven and let us in.

What is the inspiration of goodness? *Goodness* is a word that we have relegated to the nursery. We still tell the children to be good. What, then, is the inspiration of goodness in a child? Love. You may keep your boy good in the externalities by being a moral policeman. If you want to bind him to goodness through the coming years you must make of him such a boy that when he comes up to the city and sin confronts him he will say, "No, I cannot do it. It would whiten father's hair and break mother's heart!" Love is the only sufficient inspiration of goodness. "If ye *love* me, ye will keep my commandments." That is the whole philosophy of goodness, and you will never be good while you are aiming to be good because you may lose your respectability by badness. When love is in your heart, and you can say, "I cannot grieve my Father," that is the true inspiration of goodness. *Goodness is love's quality.*

Faithfulness, which may with perfect accuracy be translated "fidelity," is the good old-fashioned virtue of being true to your compact and your duty. What is equal to keeping a man true in the sense of being faithful to his compact? Nothing but love. You talk to me about infidelity–of infidelity in the marriage relationship, or in business. What is its reason? There is no love. Love makes such infidelity impossible. Where love is sentinel, I shall always be at the post of duty. Where love is the inspiration, I shall never fail in faithfulness to my compact with friend, or lover, or acquaintance. I shall never fail in my business integrity if love stands sentinel over all my actions. *Faithfulness is love's quantity.*

Meekness. What is meekness? Active humility. Unconscious humility. Believe me, it is good sometimes to use that word *unconscious* before humility to see what humility really is. Humility is always unconscious, and that is meekness. There is a so-called humility which parades itself. It is not humility. There are people who are always willing to take the lowest room at the feast, provided they come late enough for everyone to see them do it! There are people who say to me sometimes when they are talking about their work for God, "Well, yes, we are doing what we can in our humble way." And I always know they are the most conceited people for five miles around. The man who is humble does not know he is humble. Meekness is the ability to stay doing the commonplace drudgery of the carpenter's shop for eighteen years. Meekness is the ability to leave the carpenter's shop and face the crowds and deliver God's message when He so wills. Meekness is the unconsciousness of self that bears to Calvary the rugged cross in the sight of all the world. The Master said, "I am meek and lowly in heart." What was the inspiration of His toiling in the carpenter's shop, the driving power in His preaching, the reason of the Cross? There is only one answer. Love. It was love that made Him true in the commonplace of the carpenter's shop, that made Him true to the prophetic message, that made Him true to God's purpose even in the mystery of His Passion. *Meekness is love's tone.*

Temperance. What is temperance? Not merely the thing with which we so often associate the word today. Tee-totalism may be intemperate. Temperance is a greater word–no one need be anxious, I am a total abstainer–it is self-control. Tell me, what is the power of self-control? What alone is sufficient to induce anyone to attempt self-control? I think you will find by long testing of my question that it is nothing but love. A man comes to me and says, "You should not indulge in any excesses. You will injure yourself; you will spoil your chances in life." All very right and proper, but it is not a final argument. I am inclined to say to the man, "Mind your own business and leave me alone." But if a man should come to me and say, "Sir, walk carefully. You have four boys who are coming after you, and what they see you do they will do." That is my motive for self-control. Self-control is the victory of love, and the victory of love is the issue of the work of the Spirit. Do not be misled into imagining that you can control yourself in any way other than by the Spirit's interpretation of love to you and the Spirit's realization of love in your heart. That is the secret of self-control. *Temperance is love's victory.*

That analysis is rapid. I have attempted it only that I may bring you face to face with the real meaning of the statement, "The fruit of the Spirit is love." If you have love, you have all these things. Joy is its consciousness. Peace is its confidence. Longsuffering is its habit. Kindness is its activity. Goodness is its quality. Faithfulness is its quantity. Meekness is its tone. Self-control is its victory.

How shall I love? I take you back to my first word. "The fruit of the Spirit is love." I cannot love so as to have this joy, this peace, this longsuffering, this kindness, this goodness, this faithfulness, this meekness, this self-control by any way other than by handing my whole life over to that Spirit who comes to communicate the very life of Jesus that there may spring up within me the first moving of love. Someone says, "I am far away from all that." Let me ask such a one, Do you know this first movement within? Have you felt the first thrill of love? Have you felt a tenderness born within you? Then remember God's order, "First the blade, then the ear, then the full corn in the ear." This fruit of the Spirit can be perfected only through cultivation. Thank God if the first movement is in your heart. If at the back of all your thinking and planning and doing lies selfishness, then yield yourself tonight to Him who alone is able to give you the victory over self by the inflow of God's own love.

All True Grace in the Heart Summed Up in Love

Jonathan Edwards (1703–1758) was a Congregational preacher, a theologian, and a philosopher, possessing one of the greatest minds ever produced on the American continent. He graduated with highest honors from Yale in 1720, and in 1726 was ordained and served as co-pastor with his grandfather, Solomon Stoddard, in Northfield, Massachusetts. When Stoddard died in 1729, Edwards became sole pastor, a position he held until doctrinal disagreements with the church led to his resignation in 1750. He played a key role in the Great Awakening (1734–1744) and is perhaps best known for his sermon "Sinners in the Hands of an Angry God."

This sermon was taken from *Charity and Its Fruits,* by Jonathan Edwards, edited by Tryon Edwards, and published by Banner of Truth Trust, 1960.

2

All True Grace in the Heart Summed Up in Love

1 Corinthians 13:1–3

In these words we observe, first, that something is spoken of as of special importance and as peculiarly essential in Christians, which the apostle calls *charity*. And this charity, we find, is abundantly insisted on in the New Testament by Christ and his apostles—more insisted on, indeed, than any other virtue.

But, then, the word *charity*, as used in the New Testament, is of much more extensive signification than as it is used generally in common discourse. What persons very often mean by *charity* in their ordinary conversation is a disposition to hope and think the best of others and to put a good construction on their words and behavior. Sometimes the word is used for a disposition to give to the poor. But these things are only certain particular branches or fruits of that great virtue of charity that is so much insisted on throughout the New Testament. The word properly signifies "love," or "that disposition or affection whereby one is dear to another." The original Greek word, ἀγάπη, that is here translated "charity," might better have been rendered "love," for that is the proper English use of it—so that by *charity* in the New Testament is meant the very same thing as Christian love.

Though it be more frequently used for love to men, yet sometimes it is used to signify not only love to men, but love to God. So it is manifestly used by the apostle in 1 Corinthians as he explains himself in 8:1: "Knowledge puffeth up, but charity edifieth." Here the comparison is between knowledge and charity, and the preference is given to charity because knowledge puffs up, but charity edifies. And, then, in the next two verses it is more particularly explained how knowledge usually puffs up and why charity edifies, so that what is called "charity" in the first verse is called "loving God" in the third, for the very same thing is evidently spoken of in the two places. And doubtless the apostle means the same thing by charity in this thirteenth chapter that he does in the eighth. For he is here comparing the same two things together that he was there, namely, knowledge and charity. "Though . . . I have all knowledge . . . and have not charity, I am nothing" (13:2); and again, "charity never faileth: but . . . knowledge, it shall vanish away" (v. 8). So that by *charity* here, we are doubtless to understand "Christian love" in its full extent, and whether it be exercised toward God or our fellow creatures.

And this charity is here spoken of as that which is, in a distinguishing manner, the great and essential thing that will appear more fully when we observe, secondly, what things are mentioned as being in vain without it, namely, the most excellent things that ever belong to natural men–the most excellent privileges and the most excellent performances.

First, the most excellent *privileges,* such as preaching with tongues, the gift of prophecy, understanding all mysteries, faith to remove mountains, and so forth. And, secondly, the most excellent *performances,* such as giving all one's goods to feed the poor and the body to be burned, and so forth. Greater things than these no natural man ever had or did, and they are the kind of things in which men are exceedingly prone to trust. Yet the apostle declares that if we have them all, and have not charity, we are nothing. The doctrine taught, then, is this:

That all the virtue that is saving and that distinguishes true Christians from others is summed up in Christian love.

This appears from the words of the text because so many other things are mentioned that natural men may have, and the things mentioned are of the highest kind it is possible they should have, both of privilege and performance, and yet it is said they all avail nothing without this. Whereas, if any of them were saving, they would avail something without it.

And by the apostle's mentioning so many and so high things, and then saying of them all that they profited nothing without charity, we may justly conclude that there is nothing at all that avails anything without it. Let a man have what he will and do what he will, it signifies nothing without charity, which surely implies that charity is the great thing. And that everything that has not charity in some way contained or implied in it is nothing, and that this charity is the life and soul of all religion, without which all things that wear the name of virtues are empty and vain.

In speaking to this doctrine, I would first notice the nature of this divine love and then show the truth of the doctrine respecting it.

The Nature of True Christian Love

I would speak of the nature of a truly Christian love. And here I would observe, *that all true Christian love is one and the same in its principle.* It may be various in its forms and objects, and may be exercised either toward God or men, but it is the same principle in the heart that is the foundation of every exercise of a truly Christian love, whatever may be its object. It is not with the holy love in the heart of the Christian, as it is with the love of other men. Their love toward different objects may be from different principles and motives and with different views, but a truly Christian love is different from this. It is one as to its principle, whatever the object about which it is exercised. It is from the same spring or fountain in the heart, though it may flow out in different channels and diverse directions, and, therefore, it is all fitly comprehended in the one name of charity as in the text. That this Christian love is one, whatever the objects toward which it may flow forth, appears by the following things.

First, it is all *from the same Spirit* influencing the heart. It is from the breathing of the same Spirit that true Christian love arises, both toward God and man. The Spirit of God is a Spirit of love, and when the former enters the soul, love also enters with it. God is love, and he that has God dwelling in him by His Spirit will have love dwelling in him also. The nature of the Holy Spirit is love; and it is by communicating Himself in His own nature to the saints that their hearts are filled with divine charity. Hence we find that the saints are partakers of the divine nature, and Christian love is called the "love of the Spirit" (Rom. 15:30), and "love in the Spirit" (Col. 1:8), and the very bowels of love and mercy seem to signify the same thing with the "fellowship of the Spirit" (Phil. 2:1). It is that Spirit, too, that infuses love to God (Rom. 5:5); and it is by the indwelling of that Spirit that the soul abides in love to God and man (1 John 3:23–24; 4:12–13).

Second, Christian love, both to God and man, is *wrought in the heart by the same work of the Spirit.* There are not two works of the Spirit of God—one to infuse a spirit of love to God and the other to infuse a spirit of love to men. But in producing one, the Spirit produces the other, also. In the work of conversion, the Holy Spirit renews the heart by giving it a divine temper (Eph. 4:23). It is one and the same divine temper thus wrought in the heart that flows out in love both to God and man.

Third, when God and man are loved with a truly Christian love, they are both loved *from the same motives.* When God is loved aright, He is loved for His excellency and the beauty of His nature, especially the holiness of His nature. It is from the same motive that the saints are loved—for holiness' sake. And all things that are loved with a truly holy love are loved from the same respect to God. Love to God is the foundation of gracious love to men. Men are loved either because they are in some respect like God in the possession of His nature and spiritual image, or because of the relation they stand in to Him as His children or creatures–as those who are blessed of Him, or to whom His mercy is offered, or in some other way from regard to Him. Only remarking, that though Christian love be one in its principle, yet it is distinguished and variously denominated in two ways with respect to its objects and the kinds of its exercise as, for example, its degrees, and so forth.

The Virtue of True Christian Love

I now proceed *to show the truth of the doctrine that all virtue that is saving or distinguishing of true Christians is summed up in Christian love.* And, *we may argue this from what reason teaches of the nature of love.* And if we duly consider its nature, two things will appear.

First, that love will *dispose to all proper acts of respect to both God and man.* This is evident because a true respect to either God or man *consists* in love. If a man sincerely loves God, it will dispose him to render all proper respect to Him, and men need no other incitement to show each other all the respect that is due than love. Love to God will dispose a man to honor, worship, and adore Him, and heartily to acknowledge His greatness, glory, and dominion. And so it will dispose to all acts of obedience to God, for the servant that loves his master and the subject that loves his sovereign will be disposed to proper subjection and obedience. Love will dispose the Christian to behave toward God as a child to a father–amid difficulties, to resort to Him for help and put all his trust in Him just as it is natural for us in case of need or affliction to go to one that we love for pity and help. It will lead us, too, to give credit to His word and to put confidence in Him, for we are not apt to suspect the veracity of those we have entire friendship for. It will dispose us to praise God for the mercies we receive from Him, just as we are disposed to gratitude for any kindness we receive from our fellowmen that we love. Love, again, will dispose our hearts to submission to the will of God, for we are more willing that the will of those we love should be done than of others. We naturally desire that those we love should be suited and that we should be agreeable to them. True affection and love to God will dispose the heart to acknowledge God's right to govern and that He is worthy to do it, and so will dispose to submission. Love to God will dispose us to walk humbly with Him, for he that loves God will be disposed to acknowledge the vast distance between God and himself. It will be agreeable to such an one to exalt God and set Him on high above all and to lie low before Him. A true Christian delights to have God exalted on his own abasement because he loves Him. He is willing to own that God is worthy of this, and it is with delight that he casts himself in the dust before the Most High from his sincere love to Him.

And so a due consideration of the nature of love will show that it disposes men to all duties toward their neighbors. If men have a sincere love to their neighbors, it will dispose them to all acts of justice toward those neighbors, for real love and friendship always dispose us to give those we love their due and never to wrong them. "Love worketh no ill to his neighbour" (Rom. 13:10). And the same love will dispose to truth toward neighbors, and will tend to prevent all lying and fraud and deceit. Men are not disposed to exercise fraud and treachery toward those they love; for thus to treat men is to treat them like enemies, but love destroys enmity. Thus, the apostle makes use of the oneness that there ought to be among Christians, as an argument to induce them to truth between man and man (Eph. 4:25). Love will dispose to walk humbly among men, for a real and true love will incline us to high thoughts of others and to think them better than ourselves. It will dispose men to honor one another, for all are naturally inclined to think highly of those they love and to give them honor, so that by love are fulfilled these precepts: "Honour all men" (1 Peter 2:17); and "Let nothing be done through strife or vainglory, but in lowliness of mind let each esteem other better than themselves" (Phil. 2:3 KJV). Love will dispose to contentment in the sphere in which God has placed us without coveting any things that our neighbor possesses, or envying him on account of any good thing that he has. It will dispose men to meekness and gentleness in their carriage toward their neighbors, and not to treat them with passion or violence or heat of spirit but with moderation and calmness and kindness. It will check and restrain everything like a bitter spirit; for love has no bitterness in it, but is a gentle and sweet disposition and affection of the soul. It will prevent broils and quarrels and will dispose men to peaceableness and to forgive injurious treatment received from others, as it is said in Proverbs 10:12: "Hatred stirreth up strifes: but love covereth all sins."

Love will dispose men to all acts of mercy toward their neighbors when they are under any affliction or calamity, for we are naturally disposed to pity those that we love when they are afflicted. It will dispose men to give to the poor, to bear one another's burdens, and to weep with those that weep as well as to rejoice with those that do rejoice. It will dispose men to the duties they owe to one another in their several places and relations. It will dispose a people to all the duties they owe to their rulers, and to give them all that honor and subjection which are their due. And it will dispose rulers to rule the people over whom they are set justly, seriously, and faithfully, seeking their good and not any by-ends of their own. It will dispose a people to all proper duty to their ministers, to hearken to their counsels and instructions, to submit to them in the house of God, and to support and sympathize with and pray for them, as those that watch for their souls. It will dispose ministers faithfully and ceaselessly to seek the good of the souls of their people, watching for them as those that must give account. Love will dispose to suitable carriage between superiors and inferiors. It will dispose children to honor their parents and servants to be obedient to their masters, not with eye-service but in singleness of heart. It will dispose masters to exercise gentleness and goodness toward their servants.

Thus, love would dispose to all duties, both toward God and toward man. And if it will thus dispose to all duties, then it follows that it is the root and spring and, as it were, a comprehension of all virtues. It is a principle which, if it be implanted in the heart, is alone sufficient to produce all good practice. Every right disposition toward God and man is summed up in it and comes from it, as the fruit from the tree or the stream from the fountain.

Second, reason teaches that *whatever performances or seeming virtues there are without love, are unsound and hypocritical.* If there be no love in what men do, then there is no true respect to God or men in their conduct; if so, then certainly there is no sincerity. Religion is nothing without proper respect to God. The very notion of religion among mankind is that it is the creature's exercise and expression of such respect toward the Creator. But if there be no true respect or love, then all that is called religion is but a seeming show. There is no real religion in it, but it is unreal and vain. Thus, if a man's faith be of such a sort that there is no true respect to God in it, reason teaches that it must be in vain; for if there be no love to God in it, there can be no true respect to Him. From this it appears that love is always contained in a true and living faith, and that it is its true and proper life and soul, without which faith is as dead as the body is without its soul. That it is that which especially distinguishes a living faith from every other, but of this more particularly hereafter. Without love to God, again, there can be no true honor to Him. A man is never hearty in the honor he seems to render to another whom he does not love, so that all the seeming honor or worship that is ever paid without love is but hypocritical. And so reason teaches that there is no sincerity in the obedience that is performed without love. For if there be no love, nothing that is done can be spontaneous and free, but all must be forced. So without love, there can be no hearty submission to the will of God, and there can be no real and cordial trust and confidence in Him. He that does not love God will not trust Him. He never will, with true acquiescence of soul, cast himself into the hands of God or into the arms of His mercy.

And so, whatever good carriage there may be in men toward their neighbors, yet reason teaches that it is all unacceptable and in vain if at the same time there be no real respect in the heart toward those neighbors, if the outward conduct is not prompted by inward love. And from these two things taken together, namely, that love is of such a nature that it will produce all virtues, and dispose to all duties to God and men, and that without it there can be no sincere virtue, and no duty at all properly performed, the truth of the doctrine follows—that all true and distinguishing Christian virtue and grace may be summed up in love.

The Scriptures teach us that love is the sum of all that is contained in the law of God and of all the duties required in His Word. This the Scriptures teach of the Law in general and of each table of the Law in particular.

First, the Scriptures teach this *of the Law and Word of God in general.* By the Law, in the Scriptures, is sometimes meant the whole of the written Word of God as in John 10:34: "Is it not written in your law, I said, Ye are gods?" And sometimes, by the Law, is meant the five books of Moses as in Acts 24:14, where it is named with the distinction of the "law" and the "prophets." And sometimes, by the Law is meant the Ten Commandments, as containing the sum of all the duty of mankind and all that is required as of universal and perpetual obligation. But whether we take the Law as signifying only the Ten Commandments or as including the whole written Word of God, the Scriptures teach us that the sum of all that is required in it is love. Thus, when by the Law is meant the Ten Commandments, it is said in Romans 13:8, "He that loveth another hath fulfilled the law." Therefore, several of the commandments are rehearsed, and it is added in the tenth verse that "love [which leads us to obey them all] is the fulfilling of the law."

Now, unless love was the sum of what the Law requires, the Law could not be wholly fulfilled in love, for a law is fulfilled only by obedience to the sum or whole of what it contains and enjoins. So the same apostle again declares, "Now the end of the commandment is charity out of a pure heart, and of a good conscience, and of faith unfeigned" (1 Tim. 1:5). Or if we take the Law in a yet more extensive sense, as the whole written Word of God, the Scriptures still teach us that love is the sum of all required in it. In Matthew 22:40 Christ teaches that on the two precepts of loving God with all the heart and our neighbor as ourselves hang all the law and the prophets, that is, all the written Word of God. For what was then called the Law and the Prophets was the whole written Word of God that was then extant.

Second, the Scriptures teach the same thing *of each table of the Law in particular.* The command, "Thou shalt love the Lord thy God with all thy heart" (Matt. 22:37), is declared by Christ to be the sum of the first table of the Law, or the first great commandment. In verse 39 to love our neighbor as ourselves is declared to be the sum of the second table, as it is also in Romans 13:9, where the precepts of the second table of the Law are particularly specified. It is then added, "And if there be any other commandment, it is briefly comprehended in this saying, namely, Thou shalt love thy neighbour as thyself." And so in Galatians 5:14: "For all the law is fulfilled in one word, even in this; Thou shalt love thy neighbour as thyself." And the same seems to be stated in James 2:8: "If ye fulfil the royal law according to the scripture, Thou shalt love thy neighbour as thyself, ye do well." Hence, love appears to be the sum of all the virtue and duty that God requires of us, and therefore must undoubtedly be the most essential thing–the sum of all the virtue that is essential and distinguishing in real Christianity. That which is the sum of all duty must be the sum of all real virtue.

The truth of the doctrine, as shown by the Scriptures, appears from this that the apostle teaches us that "faith . . . worketh by love" (Gal.

5:6). A truly Christian faith is that which produces good works; but all the good works that it produces are by love. By this, two things are evident to the present purpose.

First, that true love *is an ingredient in true and living faith, and is what is most essential and distinguishing in it.* Love is no ingredient in a merely speculative faith, but it is the life and soul of a practical faith. A truly practical or saving faith is light and heat together–or rather light and love–while that which is only a speculative faith is only light without heat, in that it wants spiritual heat or divine love is in vain and good for nothing. A speculative faith consists only in the assent of the understanding, but in a saving faith there is also the consent of the heart. That faith which is only of the former kind is no better than the faith of devils, for they have faith so far as it can exist without love, believing while they tremble. Now, the true spiritual consent of the heart cannot be distinguished from the love of the heart. He whose heart consents to Christ as a Savior has true love to Him as such. For the heart sincerely to consent to the way of salvation by Christ cannot be distinguished from loving that way of salvation and resting in it. There is an act of choice or election in true saving faith, whereby the soul chooses Christ for its Savior and portion and accepts of and embraces Him as such. But, as was observed before, an election or choice whereby it so chooses God and Christ is an act of love–the love of a soul embracing Him as its dearest friend and portion.

Faith is a duty that God requires of everyone. We are commanded to believe, and unbelief is a sin forbidden by God. Faith is a duty required in the first table of the Law and in the first command of that table. Therefore, it will follow that it is comprehended in the Great Commandment, "Thou shalt love the Lord thy God with all thy heart." And so it will follow that love is the most essential thing in a true faith. That love is the very life and spirit of a true faith is especially evident from a comparison of this declaration of the apostle that "faith . . . worketh by love," and the last verse of the second chapter of the epistle of James, which declares that "as the body without the spirit is dead, so faith without works is dead also" (v. 26). The working, active, and acting nature of anything is the life of it, and that which makes us call a thing alive is that we observe an active nature in it. This working nature in man is the spirit that he has within him. And as his body without this spirit is dead, so faith without works is dead also. And if we would know what the working active thing in true faith is, the apostle tells us in Galatians 5:6, "Faith . . . worketh by love." So that it is love which is the active working spirit in all true faith. This is its very soul, without which it is dead as in another form he tells in the text, saying that faith without charity or love is nothing though it be to such a degree that it can remove mountains. And when he says in 1 Corinthians 13:7 that charity "believeth all things, hopeth all things," he probably refers to the great virtues of believing and hoping in the truth and grace of God, to which he compares charity in other parts of the chapter and, particularly, in the last verse, "Now abideth faith, hope, charity" (v. 13). For in the seventh verse he gives the preference to charity or love before the other virtues of faith and hope because it includes them, for he says, "[Charity] believeth all things, hopeth all things." This seems to be his meaning, and not merely, as it is vulgarly understood, that charity believes and hopes the best with regard to our neighbors. That a justifying faith, as a most distinguishing mark of Christianity, is comprehended in the great command of loving God appears, also, very plainly from what Christ says to the Jews (John 5:40–43).

Second, it is further manifest from this declaration of the apostle that "faith . . . worketh by love," *that all Christian exercises of the heart and works of the life are from love.* We are abundantly taught in the New Testament that all Christian holiness begins with faith in Jesus Christ. All Christian obedience is, in the Scriptures, called the obedience of faith; as in Romans 16:26, the gospel is said to be "made known to all nations for the obedience of faith." The obedience here spoken of is doubtless the same with that spoken of in the eighteenth verse of the preceding chapter, where Paul speaks of making "the Gentiles obedient, by word and deed." And in Galatians 2:20 he tells us "the life which I now live in the flesh I live by the faith of the Son of God," and we are often told that Christians, so far as they are Christians, "live by faith," which is equivalent to saying that all gracious and holy exercises and virtues of the spiritual life are by faith. But how does faith work these things? Why, in this place in Galatians, it is expressly said that it works whatsoever it does work *by love.* From which the truth of the doctrine follows, namely, that all that is saving and distinguishing in Christianity does radically consist and is comprehended in love.

Application

In the application of this subject, we may use it in the way of self-examination, instruction, and exhortation. *In view of it, let us examine ourselves and see* if *we have the spirit that it enjoins.* From love to God springs love to man, as says the apostle in 1 John 5:1: "Whosoever believeth that Jesus is the Christ is born of God: and every one that loveth him that begat loveth him also that is begotten of him." Have we this love to all who are the children of God? This love also leads those who possess it to rejoice in God, and to worship and magnify Him. Heaven is made up of such: "And I saw as it were a sea of glass mingled with fire: and them that had gotten the victory over the beast, and over his image, and over his mark, and over the number of his name, stand on the sea of glass, having the harps of God. And they sing the song of Moses the servant of God, and the song of the Lamb, saying, Great and marvellous are thy works, Lord God Almighty; just and true are thy ways, thou King of saints. Who shall not fear thee, O Lord, and glorify thy name? For thou only art holy: for all nations shall come and worship before thee; for thy judgments are made manifest" (Rev. 15:2–4).

Do we thus delight in God, rejoice in His worship, and in

magnifying His holy name? This love also leads those who possess it sincerely to desire and earnestly to endeavor to do good to their fellowmen: "Hereby perceive we the love of God, because he laid down his life for us: and we ought to lay down our lives for the brethren. But whoso hath this world's good, and seeth his brother have need, and shutteth up his bowels of compassion from him, how dwelleth the love of God in him? My little children, let us not love in word, neither in tongue; but in deed and in truth. And hereby we know that we are of the truth, and shall assure our hearts before him" (1 John 3:16–19). Is this spirit, which dwelt in Jesus Christ, the spirit that reigns in our hearts and is seen in our daily life?

The subject may also be of use *in the way of instruction.* First, this doctrine shows us *what is the right Christian spirit.* When the disciples, on their way to Jerusalem, desired Christ to call down fire from heaven to consume the Samaritans who would not receive Him, He told them, by way of rebuke, "Ye know not what manner of spirit ye are of" (Luke 9:55). By this we are to understand not that they did not know their own hearts, but that they did not know and truly feel what kind of spirit was proper and becoming to their character and spirit as His professed disciples, and becoming that evangelical dispensation that He had come to establish and under which they were now living. It might indeed be, and doubtless was true, that in many respects they did not know their own hearts. But what Christ here referred to was not the want of self-knowledge in general, but the particular spirit they had manifested in desiring Him to call down fire—a desire that showed not so much that they did not know what their own hearts or dispositions were, as that they did not seem to know what kind of spirit and temper was proper to the Christian dispensation that was henceforth to be established and to the Christian character of which they were to be examples. They showed their ignorance of the true nature of Christ's kingdom. It was to be a kingdom of love and peace, and they did not know but that a revengeful spirit was a proper spirit for them as His disciples, and for this it is that He rebukes them.

And, doubtless, there are many now-a-days greatly to be rebuked for this, that though they have been so long in the school of Christ and under the teachings of the gospel, yet they still remain under a great misapprehension as to what kind of a spirit a truly Christian spirit is, and what spirit is proper for the followers of Christ and the dispensation under which they live. But if we attend to the text and its doctrine, they will teach us what this spirit is, namely, that in its very essence and savor it is the spirit of divine and Christian love. This may, by way of eminence, be called *the* Christian spirit; for it is much more insisted on in the New Testament than anything that concerns either our duty or our moral state. The words of Christ whereby He taught men their duty and gave His counsels and commands to His disciples and others were spent very much on the precepts of love. As the words that proceeded out of His mouth were so full of this sweet divine virtue, He thus most manifestly commends it to us. And after His ascension, the apostles were full of the same spirit in their epistles, abundantly recommending love, peace, gentleness, goodness, bowels of compassion and kindness, directing us by such things to express our love to God and to Christ as well as to our fellowmen and, especially, to all that are His followers.

This spirit, even a spirit of love, is the spirit that God holds forth greater motives in the gospel to induce us to than to any other thing whatever. The work of redemption that the gospel makes known, above all things, affords motives to love. That work was the most glorious and wonderful exhibition of love that ever was seen or heard. Love is the principal thing that the gospel dwells on when speaking of God and of Christ. It brings to light the love eternally existing between the Father and the Son and declares how that same love has been manifested in many things: how that Christ is God's well-beloved Son, in whom He is ever well pleased; how He so loved Him that He has raised Him to the throne of the mediatorial kingdom, appointed Him to be the judge of the world, and ordained that all mankind should stand before Him in judgment. In the gospel, too, is revealed the love that Christ has to the Father, and the wonderful fruits of that love, particularly in His doing such great things and suffering such great things in obedience to the Father's will, and for the honor of His justice and law and authority, as the great moral governor. There it is revealed how the Father and Son are one in love that we might be induced, in the like spirit, to be one with them and with one another, agreeably to Christ's prayer in John 17:21–23: "That they all may be one; as thou, Father, art in me, and I in thee, that they also may be one in us: that the world may believe that thou hast sent me. And the glory which thou gavest me I have given them; that they may be one, even as we are one: I in them, and thou in me, that they may be made perfect in one; and that the world may know that thou hast sent me, and hast loved them, as thou hast loved me."

The gospel also declares to us that the love of God was from everlasting, and reminds us that He loved those that are redeemed by Christ before the foundation of the world, that He gave them to the Son, and that the Son loved them as His own. It reveals, too, the wonderful love of both the Father and the Son to the saints now in glory—that Christ not only loved them while in the world, but that He loved them to the end. And all this love is spoken of as bestowed on us while we were wanderers, outcasts, worthless, guilty, and even enemies. This is love, such as was never elsewhere known or conceived. "Greater love hath no man than this, that a man lay down his life for his friends" (John 15:13). "Scarcely for a righteous man will one die: . . . But God commendeth his love toward us, in that, while we were yet sinners, Christ died for us. . . . when we were enemies" (Rom. 5:7–10).

God and Christ appear in the gospel revelation as being clothed with love, as sitting as it were on a throne of mercy and grace, a seat of love, encompassed about with the sweet beams of love. Love is the light and glory that is around the throne on which God is seated. This seems to be intended in the vision the apostle John, that loving and loved disciple, had of God on the isle of Patmos: "And there was a rainbow round about the throne, in sight like unto an emerald" (Rev. 4:3); that is, round about the throne on which God was sitting. So that God appeared to Him, as He sat on His throne, as encompassed with a circle of exceedingly sweet and pleasant light like the beautiful colors of the rainbow, and like an emerald, which is a precious stone of exceeding pleasant and beautiful color—thus representing that the light and glory with which God appears surrounded in the gospel is especially the glory of His love and covenant grace, for the rainbow was given to Noah as a token of both of these. Therefore, it is plain that this spirit, even a spirit of love, is the spirit that the gospel revelation does especially hold forth motives and inducements to. This is especially and eminently the Christian spirit—the right spirit of the gospel.

Second, if it is indeed so, that all that is saving and distinguishing in a true Christian is summarily comprehended in love, *then professors of Christianity may in this be taught as to their experiences whether they are real Christian experiences or not.* If they are so, then love is the sum and substance of them. If persons have the true light of heaven let into their souls, it is not a light without heat. Divine knowledge and divine love go together. A spiritual view of divine things always excites love in the soul and draws forth the heart in love to every proper object. True discoveries of the divine character dispose us to love God as the supreme good. They unite the heart in love to Christ. They incline the soul to flow out in love to God's people and to all mankind. When persons have a true discovery of the excellency and sufficiency of Christ, this is the effect. When they experience a right belief of the truth of the gospel, such a belief is accompanied by love. They love Him whom they believe to be the Christ, the Son of the living God.

When the truth of the glorious doctrines and promises of the gospel is seen, these doctrines and promises are like so many cords that take hold of the heart and draw it out in love to God and Christ. When persons experience a true trust and reliance on Christ, they rely on Him with love, and so do it with delight and sweet acquiescence of soul. The spouse sat under Christ's shadow with great delight and rested sweetly under His protection because she loved Him (Cant. 2:2). When persons experience true comfort and spiritual joy, their joy is the joy of faith and love. They do not rejoice in themselves, but it is God who is their exceeding joy.

Third, this doctrine shows *the amiableness of a Christian spirit.* A spirit of love is an amiable spirit. It is the spirit of Jesus Christ–it is the spirit of heaven.

Fourth, this doctrine shows *the pleasantness of* a *Christian life.* A life of love is a pleasant life. Reason and the Scriptures alike teach us that "happy is the man that findeth wisdom" (Prov. 3:13) and that "her ways are ways of pleasantness, and all her paths are peace" (v. 17).

Fifth, hence we may learn the reason *why contention tends so much to the ruin of religion.* The Scriptures tells us that it has this tendency: "Where envying and strife is, there is confusion and every evil work" (James 3:16). And so we find it by experience. When contention comes into a place, it seems to prevent all good. And if religion has been flourishing before, it presently seems to chill and deaden it. Everything that is bad begins to flourish. And in the light of our doctrine, we may plainly see the reason of all this: for contention is directly against that which is the very sum of all that is essential and distinguishing in true Christianity, even a spirit of love and peace. No wonder, therefore, that Christianity cannot flourish in a time of strife and contention among its professors. No wonder that religion and contention cannot live together.

Sixth, hence, then, *what a watch and guard should Christians keep against envy, malice, and every kind of bitterness of spirit toward their neighbors!* For these things are the very reverse of the real essence of Christianity. And it behooves Christians, as they would not by their practice directly contradict their profession, to take heed to themselves in this matter. They should suppress the first beginnings of ill-will and bitterness and envy. They should watch strictly against all occasions of such a spirit. Strive and fight to the utmost against such a temper as tends that way. Avoid, as much as possible, all temptations that may lead to it. A Christian should at all times keep a strong guard against everything that tends to overthrow or corrupt or undermine a spirit of love. That which hinders love to men will hinder the exercise of love to God for, as was observed before, the principle of a truly Christian love is one. If love is the sum of Christianity, surely those things which overthrow love are exceedingly unbecoming Christians. An envious Christian, a malicious Christian, a cold and hardhearted Christian is the greatest absurdity and contradiction. It is as if one should speak of dark brightness or a false truth!

Seventh, hence it is *no wonder that Christianity so strongly requires us to love our enemies, even the worst of enemies* (as in Matt. 5:44), for love is the very temper and spirit of a Christian–it is the sum of Christianity. And if we consider what incitements thus to love our enemies we have set before us in what the gospel reveals of the love of God and Christ to their enemies, we cannot wonder that we are required to love our enemies, to bless them, to do good to them, and to pray for them. "That ye may be the children of your Father which is in heaven: for he maketh his sun to rise on the evil and on the good, and sendeth rain on the just and on the unjust" (v. 45).

Our subject exhorts us to seek a spirit of love, to grow in it more and more, and very much to abound in the works of love. If love is so great a thing in Christianity, so essential and distinguishing, yes, the very sum of all Christian virtue, then surely those that profess themselves Christians should live in love and abound in the works of love, for no works are so becoming as those of love. If you call yourself a Christian, where are your works of love? Have you abounded, and do you abound in them? If this divine and holy principle is in you and reigns in you, will it not appear in your life in works of love? Consider, what deeds of love have you done? Do you love God? What have you done for Him, for His glory, for the advancement of

His kingdom in the world? And how much have you denied yourself to promote the Redeemer's interest among men? Do you love your fellowmen? What have you done for them? Consider your former defects in these respects, and how becoming it is in you, as a Christian, hereafter to abound more in deeds of love. Do not make excuse that you have not opportunities to do anything for the glory of God, for the interest of the Redeemer's kingdom, and for the spiritual benefit of your neighbors. If your heart is full of love, it will find vent; you will find or make ways enough to express your love in deeds. When a fountain abounds in water, it will send forth streams. Consider that as a principle of love is the main principle in the heart of a real Christian, so the labor of love is the main business of the Christian life. Let every Christian consider these things. May the Lord give you understanding in all things, make you sensible what spirit it becomes you to be of, and dispose you to such an excellent, amiable, and benevolent life, as is answerable to such a spirit, that you may not love only "in word, neither in tongue, but in deed and in truth" (1 John 3:18).

NOTES

The Supremacy of Love

John Daniel Jones (1865–1942) served for forty years at the Richmond Hill Congregational Church in Bournemouth, England, where he ministered the Word with a remarkable consistency of quality and effectiveness, as his many volumes of published sermons attest. A leader in his denomination, he gave himself to church extension (he helped to start thirty churches), assistance to needier congregations, and he increased salaries for the clergy. He spoke at D. L. Moody's Northfield Conference in 1919.

This sermon was taken from his book, *The Greatest of These,* published in 1925 by Hodder and Stoughton.

JOHN DANIEL JONES

3

The Supremacy of Love

But now abideth faith, hope, love, these three; and the greatest of these is love. (1 Corinthians 13:13 ASV)

WITH THIS SIMPLE BUT ALMOST FATHOMLESS SENTENCE the apostle brings this exquisite hymn to a finish. He ends it on the top note. He keeps his most splendid chord for the last. Everything he has said hitherto culminates in the climax of this final statement. In the verses immediately preceding he has been asserting the superiority of love over the gifts of tongues and prophecy and knowledge–the gifts on which the Corinthians plumed and prided themselves–on the ground that, while these gifts were transient and temporary, love was permanent. "Love never faileth: but whether there be prophecies, they shall be done away; whether there be tongues, they shall cease; whether there be knowledge, it shall be done away" (v. 8 ASV). But in this verse Paul says something about love more wonderful still; he makes a claim for it more daring still. Not only is love better than such transient things as prophecy and tongues and knowledge, but of the permanent and abiding things love is the greatest and the best. For love is not the only thing that abides. Faith abides, and hope abides as well. "Now abideth faith, hope, love; but the greatest of these [even of these supreme and vital things] is *love.*" In that beautiful little booklet in which Henry Drummond expounds this chapter, he speaks of love as "the greatest thing in the world." Of course, it is that. But that description of it is an understatement. It falls short of the truth. Love is not only the greatest thing in the world, it is also the greatest thing in heaven; it is not only the greatest thing in time, it is also the greatest thing in eternity. "Now abideth faith, hope, love, these three; and the greatest of these is love."

It seems something like sacrilege to begin to examine critically a verse like this, but I should not be quite honest if I did not at least let you know that a whole school of commentators, beginning with Chrysostom, put a rather different construction upon the verse from that which is commonly received. They treat that word *now* with which the verse opens as being not the "now" of logic, but the "now" of time. *Now,* that is, in this present time, in this temporal sphere, there are three abiding things—faith, hope, and love. But in the eternal world faith and hope will disappear; there will be no further occasion for their exercise. But love will live on through all eternity. Love is superior even to faith and hope, for they will cease; but love, as Dr. Edwards says, "will survive every catastrophe." It is the interpretation embodied in that verse of a familiar hymn:

> Faith will vanish into sight
> Hope be emptied in delight.
> Love in heaven will shine more bright,
> Therefore give us love.

But though a great many scholars favor that interpretation, I am quite persuaded that the ordinary interpretation is the right one. I find it quite impossible to think that the word *abideth* when applied to "faith and hope" means "abideth for a time"; but that when applied to love it means "abideth forever." This is what Paul says: "Now abideth faith, hope, love." So far as the "abiding" is concerned, these three graces stand on the same plane. What "abiding" means for any one of them, it means for all three of them. Faith, hope, love are alike in this–that they are all permanent.

But some one may say, "What room is there for *faith* and *hope* in heaven?" What room is there for faith? Here we have to walk by faith not by sight. We have to take many things on trust. We have to *believe* that God is at work, though we cannot behold Him. We have to *believe* that all things work together for good, though they seem to us to be hopelessly tangled and awry. We have to *believe* that God is love, though oftentimes things look very unlike it. But what room is there for faith in heaven? What does the second to last verse say, "Now we see in a mirror [in a riddle]; . . . but then face to face: now I know in part; but then shall I know fully even as also I was fully known" (v. 12 ASV). "We shall see"–face to face–without the smallest wisp of cloud or shred of mist to dim our vision! There will be no longer any riddles to perplex and baffle us. We shall know! We shall know *completely;* our agonized *whys* and *wherefores* will get their answer there. Isn't that a large element in the blessedness of heaven–that the crooked will be made straight, the rough place plain, and that the glory of the Lord will be fully revealed? What room is there left for faith in that land where the Beatific Vision will be ours?

And what room is there for hope? Does not hope by its very nature seem to argue an imperfect world? That is how the case stands with us down here–we *hope* for things, but we do not always achieve them. Perhaps it would be truer to say that we never completely realize them. A certain element of disappointment seems to be inseparable from this human life of ours. We hope to accomplish certain tasks, and they are not half finished when the end comes. We hope to reach a certain height of character, and we are not halfway up the hill when the night falls. We are all of us like David in this respect–it is in our mind to do great things, but the great things never get done. And sometimes the disappointments are bitter and tragic. Think, for example, of the hopes that lie dashed and broken in the untimely graves of youth–of the hopes for England, for example, that lie buried in the graves of Rupert Brooke and young Gladstone and the Grenfells. Think of the hopes innumerable parents cherished for their lads that the brutal hand of sudden death nipped in the very bud! Hope is a bittersweet kind of thing. We could not live without it, but disappointment is its twin sister, and it argues in its very nature an uncertain life and an imperfect world. But what room is there for hope in heaven? For is not that how we picture heaven—as the place of realization and achievement? What does our old hymn say?

> There shall we feel and see and know,
> All we desired or hoped below.

"All we desired or hoped"! Is not that how we comfort ourselves in face of the shattering of our hopes for our children snatched from us in their youth—that all the promise that was in them will get its chance in heaven? "On the earth the broken arcs, in heaven the perfect round." Is not that how we comfort ourselves in face of our own imperfections and shortcomings, in face of our manifold failures and falls—falls that lay us in the very dust of shame—that in heaven we shall be completely freed from every root and fiber of sin, and that there, at last, we shall be what we want to be? Does not this Book tell us that in that day we shall be like our Lord, for we shall see Him as He is? Well, what will there be to wish for after that? What place is there for *hope* in heaven?

And yet here is the apostle declaring categorically that not love only, but faith and hope also, are abiding things. It is not love alone that "never faileth," faith and hope never fail either. They have their place in the life of heaven. They are not transient and temporary things like prophecy and tongues. They are permanent graces of the soul. "Now abideth faith, hope, love, these three." Can we understand how this should be? Well, it behooves a man to talk very diffidently when he comes to speak of conditions in the life to come, for "eye hath not seen, nor ear heard, neither have entered into the heart of man, the things which God hath prepared for them that love him" (1 Cor. 2:9 KJV). But I think we may find certain clues which—if we follow them—will help us to understand why Paul numbers faith and hope among the abiding things.

Let me once again begin with *faith.* If we understand faith to be a certain act of the intellect by which we believe in certain promises on the ground of our belief in the Promiser (which was Chrysostom's notion of faith), then, of course, faith ceases when the promises are fulfilled. Or, if we understand faith as an intellectual assent to a certain scheme of doctrine (which is an idea of faith not unfamiliar in Protestant circles), then again faith ceases because in the clear light of heaven our stumbling conceptions of truth will be swallowed up in the immediate perception of the truth itself. But is that the real meaning of faith? Does not faith in its essence mean this—trust in God, the confidence of the soul in God, the clinging of the soul to God? When we say that we walk by faith not by sight, is not that what we mean, that we trust God though we cannot see Him? We believe that in the deepest darkness He is at work, though we cannot behold Him. We stake everything on the belief that He is love, even though events challenge and seem to deny our faith. "Though he slay me, yet will I trust in him" (Job 13:15).

Well, won't there be room for faith in that sense of trust, "the clinging of the heart to God and to a living, personal Christ," as Dr. Edwards puts it, in the life of heaven? Will faith as a matter of fact not flourish more vigorously than ever? What our clear vision of God, our sight of Him face to face will do, is not to do away with faith but to intensify it. Down here faith has often a struggle for life. "Faith and unfaith can ne'er be equal powers," says Tennyson. No, perhaps not! But often, in actual experience, there is very little in it, on the balance. We are so perplexed and troubled, so puzzled and baffled by the tangled providences of life that faith almost lapses into unfaith, and the best prayer we can offer is "Lord, I believe; help thou mine unbelief" (Mark 9:24). But up yonder we shall see the meaning of things. We shall see how, all through, God has been thinking on us for our good. We shall see how trustworthy He is. And as a result of our clearer vision of God our hearts will cling to Him with a more perfect trust, with a confidence unchecked by any shadow of doubt. The difference between earth and heaven is the difference between a halting and hesitating faith and a glad and triumphant faith. But the life yonder, as here, will be one of clinging trust in God. "Now abideth faith."

And what about *hope?* I have found reason for the permanence of faith in the fact that the relation between man and God will always be that of joyful and adoring trust. I find the reason for the permanence of hope in the nature of that heaven life itself. We make a mistake if we think of all the denizens of heaven as being on the same level. "One star differeth from another star in glory," says St. Paul (1 Cor. 15:41). "So also," he adds, "is the resurrection of the dead" (v. 42). There are differences in heaven, differences of attainment and glory. There are some who are scarcely saved, and there are some who have an abundant entrance into the heavenly habitations. And this fact of difference in attainment is quite compatible with the perfect blessedness of all. Each has all the blessedness he can contain. There is fullness of joy for all, though the capacity for joy may vary in each case. And just as there are differences between the inhabitants of heaven, so there are differences in the same person at different stages. There is progress even in heaven. Our condition is not fixed forever once we reach there. "In my Father's house," said Jesus, "are many mansions" (John 14:2). "Resting-places," the word really means, and it refers to those "stations" on the great roads where travelers could get rest and refreshment before proceeding on their journey. The notions both of repose and progress, says Bishop Westcott, are in the word. We shall be moving on, so to speak, from one resting-place to another. And this idea of progress, again, is in no way inconsistent with perfection. For just exactly as in this human life of ours a person may be perfect as a child, and then perfect as a youth, and, finally, perfect as a man, so in the next world we may be continually growing and making progress and yet be perfect at each stage. And, as Dr. Edwards says, so long as progress is possible, hope has not ceased.

I suppose that in heaven, as here on earth, we shall be limited creatures. And limited creatures will always find something fresh to learn about the infinite God. With all saints we shall be forever seeking to apprehend what is the breadth and length and depth and height of the love of God. That is a task that will occupy us through all eternity, and with every fresh discovery of that love our perfection will become a deeper, fuller and richer thing.

I talked with a devoted member of this church the other day, and she found great comfort in this thought of progress. She felt so unworthy and sinful that she felt she needed some long process of purification before she was fit for the presence of God. But in the process of time she dared to hope even that final felicity might be hers. I think she forgot two things: first of all, that we are to be completely purged from our sins; and, secondly, she forgot that it is love that qualifies for the vision. "Every one that loveth is born of God" (1 John 4:7). The progress of heaven is not that we are gradually emancipated from sin and gradually gain the vision of God's face, but that as we contemplate God's love we grow in our knowledge of God and enter upon an ever-enlarging life in Him. But the progress is sure. The perfection of today will merge into the larger perfection of tomorrow. There is always something richer and better to look for. There is room for hope in the life of heaven. As Mr. Percy Ainsworth puts it, "Faith and hope will not cease to live when they no longer have to fight for their life. They are not mere adjuncts of human life. They are the fundamental terms of our personal existence and the eternal conditions of our relationship with God, and they must abide so long as God and the soul abide."

So faith and hope, as well as love, are permanent and abiding things. They have their place in the life of heaven. "Now abideth faith, hope, love, these three"—and only these three. And then the apostle adds these words: "and the greatest of these is love." Love is not simply greater than transient and temporary gifts like prophecy and tongues; it is greater than these abiding graces of the soul—faith and hope. It is the greatest thing in heaven itself. After letting his mind dwell on the various gifts on which the members of the church militantly prided themselves, and finding among them nothing comparable to love, he lifts his eyes to the contemplation of the saints in glory, and he finds that love still holds pride of place—"the greatest of these is love."

Now can we see why love is greater than either faith or hope? I am going to mention two considerations. Dr. Edwards says that St. Paul does not tell us *why* love is greater than faith and hope. St. Paul, he says, "only opens the door. To enter was reserved for St. John." But even in this very chapter the apostle gives us a hint as to why love is better than either faith or hope.

The Supremacy of Love

Without love, faith and hope are themselves imperfect. He has said as much as that in plain language about *faith.* "If I have all faith, so as to remove mountains, but have not love, I am nothing" (1 Cor. 13:2 ASV). There is a kind of faith which hasn't very much love in it. It is the kind of faith that lays hold of the merits of Christ, but has nothing in it of a spontaneous and eager delight in God. And there is a kind of hope which hasn't very much love in it. The hope that animates some Christian people is like that very materialistic hope that possessed the hearts of the first disciples, and that prompted Peter one day to say, "Lo, we have left all, and followed thee" (Luke 18:28), what then shall we get? What they hope for is reward—or, at any rate, escape from punishment. But such faith and such hope are poor and imperfect things. Both need love for their perfection. Love changes faith from trust in Christ's merits into an enthusiastic devotion to Christ Himself. Love transforms hope from hope of reward into hope of likeness to Christ, and blessed union with Him. Love is a greater thing than either faith or hope, because without love, faith and hope are themselves poor and imperfect things.

So far Paul takes us in this chapter. But it is John who supplies us with the final reason why love is greater than either faith or hope.

Love Is the Divine Grace

You cannot describe God in terms of faith or hope. "God, the all-knowing, does not *believe.* God, the all-possessing, does not hope." But you can describe God in terms of love. Indeed, those are the only terms in which you can describe Him—*God is love.* Power, wisdom, omnipresence—those are attributes of God. But love is His very nature. That is the truth blazoned for us in the cross of Jesus. We might have been doubtful of it but for that final and subduing revelation. God gave His Son to death and shame for *love.* Faith and hope are eternal things, inasmuch as they are the abiding conditions of our relationship with God. But when we love, we share God's very life. "Faith and hope are means to an end; love is the end itself." Faith and hope link us to the life of God, but love is that life itself. We enter into the very life of God, and union with God becomes a blessed reality when we love. For God is love, "and every one that loveth is born of God, and knoweth God" (1 John 4:7). That is why the apostle says, "Now abideth faith, hope, love, these three; and the greatest of these is love."

"The greatest thing in the world," says Henry Drummond. Of course it is that. It is the chief spring of such happiness as we enjoy down here. I do not say that there are not other things—such as the glory of the physical world in which we live, the companionship of books, and the delights of music and art—that add to the richness and fullness of life. But love is the abiding source of our happiness and peace. It is love—the love of father and mother, and wife and child, and friend that makes life worth having. Without love, life is not a boon but a burden.

"If a man have no friend"—it is Bacon, I think, who says it—"he may quit the stage." He probably *will* quit the stage. A man has no hold on life once love is gone. Analyze your own feelings and see if this is not so. "Why," asks Drummond, "do you want to live tomorrow? It is because there is someone who loves you and whom you want to see tomorrow and be with and love back." But who would want to live if in the wide world we had neither love nor friend? So that in the last analysis, as Drummond says, love is life, and we live only while we love. But so long as we have love, life is worthwhile.

As we grow old, the senses, which are the gateways through which other enjoyments reach us, often fail. The eyes give out, and we can be no longer ravished by the glories of nature; hearing becomes dull, and we can no longer be charmed by music and song. But old people for whom life has been in that way limited and curtailed still find it worthwhile—for though sight is gone and hearing is gone, love is still left. It is in very truth, without controversy or dispute, the greatest thing in the world. And if we only knew it, love is the healing of our world's hurt. It is not only the fountain of happiness for the individual life; it is the only possible means of quietness and peace for our world. It is not by new arrangements and changes of method we are going to bring peace and goodwill back to our disordered world, but by a change of spirit. We may make what changes of method and of organization we please, but so long as we have the same selfish spirit, strife and division, unrest and discontent will be with us still. But though our methods and our organization remained as they are—confessedly imperfect to say the least—if only we had filling the hearts of men this love that envies not, that bears, hopes, and believes all things, and that never fails, love by itself as by a stroke of a magician's wand would present us with the new world.

Love is not only the best thing in life and the healing of the world's hurt, it is *the Alpha and Omega of religion.* You can sum up religion in terms of love. For what is the final and ultimate source of this Christian faith of ours? What is its primal and original fount? Why, the infinite love of God. "God so loved the world" (John 3:16). Everything begins with that uncreated and eternal love. But for that love there would have been for lost and wayward men no redemption or salvation at all. And when does that salvation provided by the uncreated love of God become a reality in individual experience? When does religion begin in you and me? When love for God awakens in these hearts of ours. When looking into the face of Jesus—that torn and scarred visage—we say with Peter, "Lord, thou knowest all things; thou knowest that I love thee" (John 21:17). And how does religion show itself? What is its practical effect in life? And again I say, "Love." By this know we that we have passed out of death into life—because we love the brethren. Pure and undefiled religion before God and the Father is this: to visit the fatherless and widows in their affliction and to keep oneself unspotted from the world. We are sometimes half inclined to identify religion with creeds and doctrines, and rites and ceremonies. We are wrong there. Creeds and doctrines, rites and ceremonies are not of the essence of religion. But you can sum religion up in terms of love. It begins in eternity with the love of God; it starts in you and me, when our love responds to that mighty love of God; it reveals itself in the loving life.

"The greatest thing in the world"? Yes, it is that. But it is more than that. It is the greatest thing in heaven as well. Of all the abiding things, love is supreme. "Now abideth faith, hope, love, these three; and the greatest of these is love." It is the very life of heaven, for it is the nature of God Himself. Heaven is the abode of the loving. Love is the qualification for entrance, and the selfish and unloving find no admittance. The test of entrance into the Celestial City, as Drummond puts it, "is not religiousness, but love. Not what I have done, not what I have believed, not what I have achieved, but how I have discharged the common charities of life." "Come, ye blessed . . . inherit the kingdom prepared for you from the foundation of the world" (Matt. 25:34). Who are these people? They are just the loving—the people who fed the hungry, clothed the naked, visited the sick, and who out of sheer love went about doing good. We all want to wing home to that blessed country at the finish.

Well, have you got love? It is of no use talking about your orthodoxy and your church membership and the rest of it. You will not be asked questions about those things—but have you got love, this sacred love for God and man that reveals itself in a loving life? You may have faith so as to remove mountains, yet if you have no love be nothing at all. Love is the one thing needful. It is the very spirit of Jesus. And if we have not the spirit of Christ, we are none of His. If you have not got it—do you desire it? How can love be gotten? Where can love be kindled? I will tell you. At the cross of Jesus. Gaze at that cross long enough and realize that it was for you He hung and suffered there—and love will be born. The love of Christ will constrain you (see 2 Cor. 5:14) once you realize that the Son of God loved you and gave Himself up for you.

NOTES

The Fruit of the Spirit: Joy

Charles Haddon Spurgeon (1834–1892) is undoubtedly the most famous minister of the nineteenth century. Converted in 1850, he united with the Baptists and soon began to preach in various places. He became pastor of the Baptist church in Waterbeach, England, in 1851, and three years later he was called to the decaying Park Street Church, London. Within a short time, the work began to prosper, a new church was built and dedicated in 1861, and Spurgeon became London's most popular preacher. In 1855, he began to publish his sermons weekly; today they make up the fifty-seven volumes of *The Metropolitan Tabernacle Pulpit*. He founded a pastor's college and several orphanages.

This sermon was taken from *The Metropolitan Tabernacle Pulpit,* volume 27.

4

The Fruit of the Spirit: Joy

But the fruit of the Spirit is . . . joy. (Galatians 5:22)

OBSERVE, "THE *fruit* OF THE SPIRIT," for the product of the Spirit of God is one. As some fruits are easily divisible into several parts, so you perceive that the fruit of the Spirit, though it be but one, is threefold, no, it makes three times three–"love, joy, peace; longsuffering, gentleness, goodness, faith, meekness, temperance–all one. Perhaps *love* is put first not only because it is a right royal virtue, nearest akin to the divine perfection, but because it is a comprehensive grace and contains all the rest. All the commandments are fulfilled in one word, and that word is *love*. All the fruits of the Spirit are contained in that one most sweet, most blessed, most heavenly, most Godlike grace of love. See that you abound in love to the great Father and all His family. For if you fail in the first point, how can you succeed in the second? Above all things, put on love, which is the bond of perfectness. As for joy, if it be not the first product of the Spirit of God, it is next to the first, and we may be sure that the order in which it is placed by the inspired apostle is meant to be instructive. The fruit of the Spirit is love first, as comprehensive of the rest, then joy arising out of it. It is remarkable that joy should take so eminent a place; it attains to the first three and is but one place lower than the first. Look at it in its high position, and if you have missed it or have depreciated it, revise your judgment and endeavor with all your heart to attain to it. For depend upon it, this fruit of the Spirit is of the utmost value. This morning, as I can only speak upon one theme, I leave *love* for another occasion and treat only the word *joy*. May its divine author, the Holy Ghost, teach us how to speak of it to our profit and His own glory.

It is quite true that the Spirit of God produces sorrow, for one of His first effects upon the soul is holy grief. He enlightens us as to our lost condition, convincing us of sin, of righteousness, and of judgment. The first result upon our heart is astonishment and lamentation. Even when we look to Christ by the work of the Spirit, one of the first fruits is sorrow: "They shall look upon [him] whom they have pierced, and they shall mourn for him, . . . and shall be in bitterness for him, as one that is in bitterness for his firstborn" (Zech. 12:10). But this sorrow is not the ultimate object of the Spirit's work, it is a means to an end. Even as the travail of the mother leads up to the joy of birth, so do the pangs of repentance lead up to the joy of pardon and acceptance. The sorrow is, to use a scriptural figure, the blade, but the full corn in the ear is joy; sorrow helps on the fruit, but the fruit itself is joy. The tears of godly grief for sin are all meant to sparkle into the diamonds of joy in pardoning love.

This teaches us, then, that we are not to look upon bondage as being the object of the work of the Spirit of God or the design of the Lord in a work of grace. Many are under bondage to the Law: they attempt to keep the commands of God, not out of love but from slavish fear. They dread the lash of punishment and tremble like slaves. But to believers it is said, "Ye are not under the law, but under grace" (Rom. 6:14); and "Ye have not received the spirit of bondage again to fear; but ye have received the Spirit of adoption, whereby we cry, Abba, Father" (8:15). To be in bondage under the Law, to be afraid of being cast away by God and visited with destruction on account of sin after we have trusted in Jesus, this is not the work of the Spirit of God in believers but the black offspring of unbelief or ignorance of the grace of God that is in Christ Jesus our Lord.

Neither is a painful dread or a servile terror a fruit of the Spirit. Many worship even the Lord Jesus Himself at a distance. They know not that believers are "a people near unto him" (Ps. 148:14). They are afraid of God, but they never delight in Him; they attend to worship, not because they rejoice in it but because they think it must be done. Their secret feeling is, "What a weariness it is," but necessity compels. They know nothing of a child's joy in sure and full forgiveness, spoken by the Father's own lips as He pressed them to His bosom. His kiss was never warm upon their cheek, the ring was never on their finger, nor the best robe upon their shoulder. The music and the dancing of the joyous family, who are in harmony with the father's joy over the lost son, have never charmed their ears. They are still under dread, which is the fruit of superstition rather than "the fruit of the Spirit." Many things they do and suffer, and all in vain. If the Son did but make them free they would be free indeed.

I know some whom I am very far from despising, but whom on the contrary I greatly value, whose religion, sincere as I know it is, is sadly tinged with gloomy colors. They are afraid of assurance, for they dread presumption. They dare not speak of their own salvation with the certainty with which the Bible saints were wont to speak of it. They always say, "I hope" and "I trust." They would seem to be total abstainers from joy. They are suspicious of it lest it should be carnal excitement or visionary hope. They hang their heads like bulrushes and go mourning all their days, as if the religion of Christ knew no higher festival than a funeral and all its robes were the garments of despair. Friends, despondency is not the fruit of the Spirit. Make no mistake, depression is frequently the fruit of indigestion, satanic temptation, unbelief, or some harbored sin, but "the fruit of the Spirit is . . . joy." Constantly looking within your own self instead of looking alone to Christ is enough to breed misery in any heart. I have also known gloomy expressions to be the fruit of affectation, the fruit of the unwise imitation of some undoubtedly good person who was of a downcast spirit. Some of the best of men have had a melancholy turn, but they would have been better men if this had been overcome. Imitate their many virtues; take the pot of ointment and pick out the dead fly. O my friends, look well to it that you bring forth the genuine, holy, sacred, delicious fruit of the Spirit, which in one of its forms is *joy*. Do not covet the counterfeit of earthly joy, but seek to the good Spirit to bear the true fruit in you.

Joy Is Brought Forth

In speaking upon this joy, I shall notice, first, the fact that *it is brought forth*. Brethren, the Spirit of God is not barren. If He be in you, He must and will inevitably produce His own legitimate fruit, and "the fruit of the Spirit is . . . joy."

We know this to be the fact because *we ourselves are witnesses of it*. Joy is our portion, and we are cheered and comforted in the Savior. "What!" say you, "are we not depressed and sorrowful at times?" Yes, verily. Yet what Christian man or woman among us would make an exchange with the happiest of all worldlings? Your lot is somewhat hard, my friend, and sometimes your spirit sinks within you. But do you not count yourself to be, even at your worst, happier than the worldling at his best? Come, would you not take your poverty, even with your mourning, rather than accept his wealth with all his hilarity and give up your hope in God? I am persuaded you would. You would not change your blest estate for a monarch's crown. Well, then, that which you would not change is a good thing and full of joy to your heart.

We experience extraordinary joys at times. Some are of an equable temperament, and they are almost to be envied, for a stream of gentle joy always glides through their spirit. Others of us are of a more excitable character, and, consequently, we fall very flat at times. But then we have our high days and holidays and mounting times, and then we out soar the wings of eagles. Heaven itself can hardly know more ecstatic joy than we have occasionally felt. We shall be vessels of greater capacity there, but even here we are at times full to the brim of joy—I mean the same joy that makes heaven so glad. At times God is pleased to inundate the spirit with a flood of joy, and we are witnesses that "happy is that people, whose God is the LORD" (Ps. 144:15). We do not dance before the ark every day, but when we do, our joy is such as no worldling can understand. It is far above and out of his sight.

Besides our own witness, the *whole history of the church goes to show that God's people are a joyful people.* I am sure that if in reading the history of the first Christian centuries you are asked to point out the men to be envied for their joy, you would point to the believers in Jesus. There is a room in Rome that is filled with the busts of the emperors. I have looked at their heads. They look like a collection of prizefighters and murderers, and scarcely could I discover on any countenance a trace of joy. Brutal passions and cruel thoughts deprived the lords of Rome of all chance of joy. There were honorable exceptions to this rule. But taking them all round, you would look in vain for moral excellence among the Caesars, and lacking this thing of beauty they missed that which is a joy.

Turn now to the poor, hunted Christians and read the inscriptions left by them in the catacombs. They are so calm and peaceful that you say instinctively—a joyous people were wont to gather here. Those who have been most eminent in service and in suffering for Christ's sake have been of a triumphant spirit, dauntless because supported by an inner joy. Their calm courage made them the wonder of the age. The true Christian is a different type of personhood from the self-indulgent tyrant; there is almost as much advance from the coarseness of vice to the beauty of holiness as there is from the chimpanzee to the man. I do not know how much Tiberias and Caligula and Nero used to sing—happy men they certainly were not. I can hardly imagine them singing, except at their drunken orgies, and then in the same tone as tigers growl. But I do know that Paul and Silas sang praises unto God with their feet in the stocks, and the prisoners heard them. I know also that this was the mark of the Christians of the first age, that, when they assembled on the Lord's day, it was not to groan but to sing praises to the name of one *Christos,* whom they worshiped as a God. High joys were common, then, when the Bridegroom comforted His bride in the dens and caves of the earth. Those pioneers of our holy faith were destitute, afflicted, tormented, yet were they people of whom the world was not worthy, and people who counted it all joy to suffer persecution for Christ's sake. Now, if in the very worst times God's people have been a happy people, I am sure they are so now. I would appeal to the biographies of men of our own day, and challenge question as to the statement that their lives have been among the most desirable of human existences for they possessed a joy that cheered their sorrows, blessed their labors, sweetened their trials, and sustained them in the hour of death.

With some Christians this fruit of the Spirit is perpetual, or almost so. I do not doubt that many walk with God as Enoch did throughout the whole day of their lives, always peaceful and joyful in the Lord. I have met with some dear brothers and sisters of that kind whose breath has been praise, whose lives have been song. How I envy them and chide my own heart that I cannot always abide in their choice condition. It is to be accomplished, and we will press forward until we are "always rejoicing." But with others joy is not constant, and yet it is frequent. David had his mourning times, when tears were his meat day and night, and yet God was his exceeding joy. How thankful we ought to be for the portrait of David's inner self, which is presented to us in the book of Psalms. With all his downcastings, what joys he had. David was, on the whole, a joyous man. His book of Psalms has in it lyrics of delight—the gladdest hymns that ever leaped from human tongues. David is, I believe, the type of a great majority of the people of God, who if not "always rejoicing" are yet often so. Please to recollect that the utmost fullness of joy could hardly be enjoyed always in this mortal life. I believe that the human frame is not in this world capable of perpetual ecstasy. Look at the sun, but look not too long lest you be blinded by excess of light. Taste of honey, but eat not much of it, or it will no longer please the palate. Let your ear be charmed with the "Hallelujah" chorus, but do not dream that you could endure its harmonies all the hours of the day, before long you would cry out for eloquent pauses and sweet reliefs of silence. Too much even of delight will weary our feeble hearts, and we shall need to come down from the mount. Our bodies require a portion of sleep, and that which is inevitable to the flesh has its likeness in the spirit. It must be quiet and still.

I believe it is inevitable also, more or less, that the loftiest joy should be balanced by a sinking of heart. I do not say that depression is certain to follow delight, but usually some kind of faintness comes over the finite spirit after it has been lifted up into communion with the Infinite. Do not, therefore, set too much store by your own feelings as evidences of grace. "The fruit of the Spirit is . . . joy," but you may not at this moment be conscious of joy. Trees are not always bearing fruit, and yet "their substance is in them when they lose their leaves." Some young people say, "Oh, we know we are saved because we are so happy." It is by no means a sure evidence, for joy may be carnal, unfounded, unspiritual. Certain Christians are afraid that they cannot be in a saved state because they are not joyous, but we are saved by faith and not by joy. I was struck with the remark of Ebenezer Erskine when he was dying, and someone said to him, "I hope you have now and then a *blink* to bear up your spirit under affliction." He promptly replied, "I know more of *words* than of *blinks.*" That is to say, he had rather trust a promise of God than his own glimpses of heaven, and so would I. The Word of God is a more sure testimony to the soul than all the raptures a man can feel. I would sooner walk in the dark and hold hard to a promise of my God than trust in the light of the brightest day that ever dawned. Precious as the fruit is, do not put the fruit where the root should be. Please do recollect that. Joy is not the root of grace in the soul, it is the fruit and must not be put out of its proper position.

"The fruit of the Spirit is . . . joy," and it is brought forth in believers not alike in all, but to all believers there is a measure of joy.

Joy Is of a Singular Character

Secondly, this joy is of a singular character. It is singular for this reason, that *it often ripens under the most remarkable circumstances.* As I have already said, the highest joy of Christians has often been experienced in their times of greatest distress. Tried believers have been happy when smarting under pain or wasting away with disease. Sickbeds have been thrones to many saints. They have almost feared to come out of the furnace, because the presence of the Lord in the midst of the fire has made it none other than the gate of heaven to their souls. Saints in poverty have been made exceedingly rich, and when they have eaten a dry crust they have found a flavor with it that they never discovered in the dainties of their abundance. Many children of God, even when driven away from the outward means of grace, have nevertheless enjoyed such visits of God, such inlets of divine love, that they have wondered whence such joy could come. In the wilderness waters leap forth and streams in the desert. Believers are not dependent upon circumstances. Their joy comes not from what they have but from what they are, not from where they are but from whose they are, not from what they enjoy but from that which was suffered for them by their Lord. It is a singular joy, then, because it often buds, blossoms, and ripens in winter time. When the fig tree does not blossom and there is no herd in the stall, God's Habakkuks rejoice in the God of their salvation.

It is a singular joy, too, because *it is quite consistent with spiritual conflict.* He that is an heir of heaven may cry, "O wretched man that I am! who shall deliver me from the body of this death?" (Rom. 7:24). Yet, before the sigh is over, he may sing,

"I thank God, through Jesus Christ our Lord." Sorrowful, yet always rejoicing; struggling, yet always victorious; cast down, but not destroyed; persecuted, but not forsaken; troubled, and yet all the while triumphant; such is the mingled experience of the saints. Oh, this is the wondrous grace, this joy that can live side by side with conflict of the sorest sort.

This joy is special because *at times it is altogether beyond description.* One who was of a sober disposition called it "joy unspeakable and full of glory." "Full of glory"! That is a wonderful expression. A drop of glory is sweet, but, oh, to taste a joy that is full of glory—is that possible here? Yes, and some of us bear witness that it is so. We have felt joy that we dare not tell and could not tell if we dared. Men would turn again and remind us, condemning us as utterly fanatical or out of our minds if we were to cast these pearls before them. But, oh, if they could guess what delicious draughts are held within the jeweled chalice of divine communion, they would be ready to wade through hell itself to drink from it. Our joy is altogether unspeakable joy at times.

One more singularity there is in it, for *it is all the while solid, thoughtful, rational joy.* The joy of the ungodly is like the crackling of thorns under a pot—noisy, flashy, but soon over. The ungodly man feels merry, but really if you come to look into his mirth there is nothing in it but flame without fuel, sparkle without solidity. But the Christian's joy is such that he has as much reason for it as if it were a deduction from mathematics. He has just as much right to be joyful as he has to eat his own bread. He is certain of his pardon, for God has told him that a believer in Christ is not condemned. He is sure of his acceptance, for he is justified by faith. He knows that he is secure, for Christ has given him eternal life and said that His sheep shall never perish. He is happy, not for causes at which he guesses, but by infallible reasons plainly revealed in God's Word. This makes him joyful in the Lord when others wonder that he is so, for he perceives arguments for happiness that are unknown to the thoughtless crowd.

That word *joyful* is a very sweet and clear one. *Happiness* is a very dainty word, but yet it is somewhat insecure because it begins with a "hap," and seems to depend on a chance which may happen to the soul. We say "happy-go-lucky," and that is very much the world's happiness. It is a kind of thing that may hap and may not hap. But there is no hap in the fruit of the Spirit that is joy. When we are joyful or full of joy, and that of the best kind, we are favored indeed. No man takes this joy from us, and a stranger intermeddles not within it. It is a celestial fruit, and earth cannot produce its like.

Joy Is Experienced

Thirdly, I now would refresh your memories and by the help of the Spirit of God bring back former joys to you. *This joy is experienced by the Christian under various forms.* Sometimes he experiences it in *hearing the word.* It is written concerning Samaria that there was great joy in that city because Philip went down and preached the gospel to them. Blessed are the people that know the joyful sound. However, joy of hearing lies in *believing* what you hear. We get joy and peace in believing. When you get a grip of the word, when the glad tidings become a message to your own soul, and the Spirit speaks it to your own heart, then you say, "Go on, man of God. Your sermon will not be too long today, for the Lord is laying it home to my soul." The reason why people grumble at long sermons often is because they do not feed on them. Very seldom the hungry man murmurs at having too big a meal. It is a delightful thing to hear the Word faithfully preached. Have you not sometimes exclaimed, "How beautiful upon the mountains are the feet of him that bringeth good tidings" (Isa. 52:7)? That is one occasion of joy.

But what joy there is, dear friends, in *the salvation of God* when we heartily receive it. Oh, how we bless the God of our salvation, and how we praise Him that He has saved us from our sins and from the wrath to come by giving us everlasting consolation and good hope through grace by the sacrifice of His dear Son. Frequently we revel in *the privileges of the covenant.* The joy of my heart when I think of the doctrine of *election* is quite inexpressible. That hymn which begins—

> In songs of sublime adoration and praise,
> Ye pilgrims to Zion who press,
> Break forth, and extol the great Ancient of days,
> His rich and distinguishing grace—

is often with me, and makes my heart merry.

Then the doctrine of *redemption,* of which I tried to speak last Sabbath day, how joyous it is! What bliss to know that the Redeemer lives. "Unto you therefore which believe he is precious" (1 Peter 2:7), and a fullness of joy flows forth at every remembrance of Him. Then that doctrine of *justification* is the marrow of joy. Oh, to think that we are just in the sight of God through Jesus Christ. All the doctrines of grace, especially that of *final perseverance,* are joyful truths. I protest that, if you take final perseverance from me, you have robbed the Bible of one of its crowning attractions. Jesus has not given us a transient salvation, but His salvation shall be forever. I will quote again those matchless words of His: "I give unto my sheep eternal life, and they shall never perish, neither shall any pluck them out of my hand." Honey flows here as in the wood of Jonathan; put it to your mouth and your eyes shall be enlightened. The joy of God's people when they can get half-an-hour alone and sit down and crack a dish of those nuts called the doctrines of grace is such as philosophical worldlings might well desire. The modern gospel has no such wines on the lees well refined.

But, friends, our grandest joy is in *God* Himself. Paul says, "And not only so, but we also joy in God through our Lord Jesus Christ" (Rom. 5:11). Oh, to think of the great Father! What a melting of spirit comes over the child of God if at midnight he looks up at the stars and considers the heavens and cries, "What is man, that thou art mindful of him?" (Ps. 8:4; Heb. 2:6). To think that he is not only mindful of us, but that he has taken us to be His sons and daughters! To feel the Spirit within our heart crying, "Abba, Father! Abba, Father!" Oh, this is joy in the most profound sense.

How sweet to think of Jesus Christ the Son, the glorious incarnate God, the surety, the satisfaction, the representative, the all in all of His people. We joy in God through our Lord Jesus Christ. Nor do we miss the joy of the Spirit when we know that He dwells in us. He sanctifies us, comforts us, and guides us on the road to heaven. Oh friends, this is a sea of bliss, the infinite deeps of the eternal godhead! Leap from all your miseries into this sea of glory. Plunge into the joy of your Lord.

This being so, we have a joy in all God's *ordinances:* "With joy shall ye draw water out of the wells of salvation" (Isa. 12:3). What a joy prayer is. I hope you find it so. The Lord has said, "[I will] make them joyful in my house of prayer" (56:7). And what a joy it is to get answers to our petitions, even as our Lord says, "Ask, and ye shall receive, that your joy may be full" (John 16:24). Has not your joy been full, until your eyes have been dimmed with tears and you have not hardly dared to tell how wondrously God has answered you? The mercy seat is lit up with joy. What a joyous ordinance is that of praise! We come up to the sanctuary and bring our offering to God and present Him our oblation, just as the Jew of old brought his bullock or his lamb, and we joyfully present our gift to the Most High. Then we begin to sing His praises, and our joy is the chief musician upon our stringed instruments. How our spirits rise as we adore the Lord! The amount of happiness felt in this tabernacle when we have been singing to the Lord can never be measured. For my own part, I have seemed to stand just outside the wall of the New Jerusalem joining in the hymns that are sung within the gates of the eternal city. One joy note has helped another, and the volume of sound has affected every part of our being and stirred us up to vehemence of joy.

And oh, what joy there is in coming to the Lord's Table! May we experience it tonight as we have often done before.

The Lord is known to us in the breaking of bread and that knowledge is blissful.

But I have scarcely begun the list yet, for we have a great joy in *the salvation of other people.* Perhaps one of the choicest delights we know is when we partake in the joy of the Good Shepherd over His lost sheep when He calls us together, for we also are His friends and His neighbors, and bids us rejoice that He has found the sheep that was lost. Especially do we joy and rejoice if the poor wanderer has been brought back by our means. The jewels of an emperor are nothing compared with the riches we possess in winning a soul for Christ. "They that sow in tears shall reap in joy" (Ps. 126:5). The joy of harvest is great, the joy of the man who comes again rejoicing, bringing his sheaves with him. Do you know this joy, brothers and sisters? If you do not, rouse yourselves, and may this sweet fruit of the Spirit yet be yours.

Oh, the joy of seeing Christ exalted! John the Baptist said, "He must increase, but I must decrease." He called himself the Bridegroom's friend and rejoiced greatly in the Bridegroom's joy. We can sympathize with him when we can bring about a marriage between Christ and any poor soul and help to put the ring on the finger. The joy we feel is of the purest and loveliest order, for it is unselfish and refined. Let Jesus be exalted, and we ask no more. If he reigns, we reign; if he is lifted up, our hearts are more than satisfied.

If we ever become perfect in heart, we shall joy in *all the divine will,* whatever it may bring us. I am trying, if I can, to find a joy in rheumatism, but I cannot get up to it yet. I have found a joy when it is over—I can reach that length—and I can and do bless God for any good result that may come of it. But when the pain is on *me,* it is difficult to be joyous about it. So I conclude that my sanctification is very incomplete, and my conformity to the divine will is sadly imperfect. Oh, the splendor of God's will! If a man were as he ought to be, God's will would charm him, and he would not wish for the smallest change in it. Poverty, sickness, bereavement, death are all to be rejoiced in when our will is merged in the will of God. What! Would you alter God's infinitely wise appointment? Would you wish to change the purpose of unerring love? Then you are not wholly reconciled to God. For when the head gets quite right, the heart climbs where Paul was when he said, "We glory in tribulations also; knowing that tribulation worketh patience; And patience experience" (Rom. 5:3–4). It needs a Samson to kill the lion of affliction, and you cannot get honey out of it until it is conquered; but we might all be Samsons if we would but lay hold on the strength of God by faith.

Dear brothers and sisters, the list of joys, which I am even now only commencing, contains the joy of *an easy conscience,* the joy of feeling you have done right before God, the joy of knowing that your object, though misunderstood and misrepresented, was God's glory. This is a jewel to wear on one's breast—a quiet conscience. Then there is the joy of communion with Christ, the joy of fellowship with His saints, the joy of drinking deep into Christ's spirit of self-sacrifice. There, too, is the joy of expecting His glorious advent when He and His saints shall reign upon the earth, and the joy of being *with Him forever.* The joy of *heaven,* the joy of which we have been singing just now. These joys are countless, but I will pause here and leave you to make a fuller catalog when you are at home. May the Holy Spirit not only refresh your memories concerning old joys, but bring forth out of his treasury new delights that your joy may be full.

Joy May Be Checked in Its Growth

I must notice, in the fourth place, *that this fruit of the Spirit may be checked in its growth.* Some of you may have muttered while I have been speaking of this joy, "I do not know much about it." Perhaps not, friend. Shall I tell you why? Some people are too full of the joy of the world, the joy of getting on in business, the joy of a numerous family, the joy of health, the joy of wealth, the joy of human love, or the joy that comes of the pride of life. These joys may be your idols, and you know the joy of the Lord will not stand side by side with an idolatrous delight in the things of this world. See to that. Dagon must fall if the ark of the Lord is present. The world must lose its charms if you are to joy in Christ Jesus.

Our joy is sadly diminished by our unbelief. If you will not believe neither shall you be established. Ignorance will do the same to a very large extent. Many a Christian has a thousand reasons for joy which he knows nothing of. Study the Word and ask for the teaching of the Spirit of God that you may understand it, so shall you discover wells of delight. Joy is diminished, also, by walking at a distance from God. If you get away from the fire, you will grow cold. The warmest place is right in front of it, and the warmest place for a believing heart is close to Christ in daily fellowship with Him.

It may be that sin indulged is spoiling our joy. "This little hand of mine," as Mr. Whitefield once said, "can cover up the sun as far as my eyes are concerned." You have only to lift a naughty, rebellious hand, and you can shut out the light of God Himself. Any known sin will do it. Trifling with sin will prove a kill-joy to the heart.

I believe that many lose the joy of the Lord because they do not put it in the right place. See where it lives. Look at the text: "The fruit of the Spirit is love, joy, and peace." There joy stands in the center. "Love" is on one side and "peace" on the other. Find a man who never loved anybody and you have found a joyless man. This man's religion begins and ends with looking to his own safety. The only point he longs to know is, is he himself saved? He never knows joy, poor creature. How can he? As to peace, where is it? He has none, because wherever he goes he growls, grumbles, snarls, and barks at everybody. There is no peace where he is; he is always quarrelling. Then he says, "I have little joy." He does not live in the right house for joy. Joy dwells at number 2. "Love" is number 1. "Joy" is number 2; "peace" is number 3. If you pull down either of the houses on the side, number 2 in the middle will tumble down. Joy is the center of a triplet, admit you must have it so or not at all: "love, joy, peace." Thus have I shown how the growth of joy can be checked. I pray you do not allow such an evil thing to be wrought in your heart.

Joy Is to Be Carefully Cultivated

But, lastly, *it ought to be carefully cultivated.* There is an obligation upon a Christian to be happy. Let me say it again: there is a responsibility laid upon a Christian to be cheerful. It is not merely an invitation, but it is a command: "Be glad in the LORD, and rejoice, ye righteous" (Ps. 32:11). "Rejoice in the Lord alway: and again I say, Rejoice" (Phil. 4:4). Gloomy Christians, who do not resist despondency and strive against it, but who go about as if midnight had taken up its abode in their eyes and an everlasting frost had settled on their souls, are not obeying the commands of God. The command to rejoice is as undoubted a precept of God as to love the Lord with all your heart. The vows of God are upon you, O believer, and they bind you to be joyful.

In this joyfulness you shall find many great advantages. First, it is a great advantage in itself to be happy. Who would not rejoice if he could? Who would not rejoice when God commands him? Rejoicing will nerve you for life's duties. "The joy of the LORD is your strength" (Neh. 8:10). A man who goes about Christ's work in an unwilling, miserable spirit will do it badly and feebly. He may do it earnestly, but there will be no life or energy about him. Hear how the sailors when they pull the rope will shout and sing and work all the better for their cheery notes. I do not believe our soldiers would march to battle with half their present courage if they tramped along in silence. Beat the drums! Let the trumpet sound forth its martial note! Every man is eager for the fray while soul-stirring music excites him. Let your heart make music to God, and you will fight valiantly for the kingdom of your Lord.

Holy joy will also be a great preventive. The man who feels the joy of the Lord will not covet worldly joy. He will not be tempted to make a god of his possessions or of his talents or of anything else. He will say, "I have joy in God. These things I am very thankful for, but they are not my joy." He will not crave the aesthetic in worship, for his joy will be in God and His truth and not in external forms. Some people's idea of joy in religion lies in fine singing, charming music, pretty dresses, splendid architecture, or showy eloquence. They need this because they do not know the secret joy of the Lord. For when that holy passion reigns within, you may sit inside four white-washed walls and not hear a soul speak for a whole hour and a-half, and yet you may have as intense a joy as if you listened to the most earnest oratory or the sweetest song.

Joy in God is suitable to our condition!

> Why should the children of a king
> Go mourning all their days?

What are we at now, some of us? We have been hanging our harps on the willows. Let us take them down. The willow boughs will bend. Thank God, we did not break the harps, though we did hang them there. Let us get into our right position. Children of the happy God should themselves be happy.

Joy is certainly the best preparation for the future. We are going where, if we learn to groan never so deeply, our education will be lost, for melancholy utterances are unknown up there. We are going where, if we learn to sing with sacred joy, our education will be useful. For the first thing we shall hear when we get into heaven will undoubtedly be, "Hallelujah to God and the Lamb." If we have been joyful on earth, we shall say, "Ah, I am at home here." To enter heaven with a joyful soul is only to rise from downstairs to the upper chamber where the music knows no discord. It is the same song in both places, "Unto him that loved us, and washed us from our sins in his own blood" (Rev. 1:5).

Joy in the Lord will be very helpful to you as to usefulness. I am sure a Christian man's usefulness is abridged by dreariness of spirit. What nice Sunday school teachers some Christians I know of would make! "Come ye children, hearken unto me, I will teach you the miseries of religion." The dear brother begins by telling the children about the Slough of Despond, and Giant Despair, and the Valley of the Shadow of Death. He wonders when he gets home that the dear children are not attracted to the ways of godliness. Are they likely to be? A member of a church who has no joy of the Lord is little likely to encourage or influence others. They edge off from him. Even those who try to comfort him find it is to no purpose, and so they give him a wide berth. You hear him stand up to address an assembly of believers to tell his experience, and after a very little of it you feel you have had enough. Those who drink wine will tell you that half a dozen drops of vinegar are more than they want in a glass of wine, and those who carry the cruet about wherever they go are not choice company. I do not find fault with gloomy souls, but they might be more useful if they could live more in the sunlight.

The joy of the Lord is the most injurious to Satan's empire of anything. I am of the same mind as Luther, who, when he heard any very bad news, used to say, "Come, let us sing a psalm, and spite the Devil." There is nothing like it. Whenever anything happens that is rough and ugly, and seems to injure the kingdom of Christ, say to yourself, "Bless the Lord, glory be to his name." If the Lord has been dishonored by the falling away of a false professor or the failure of the ministry in any place, let us give Him all the more honor ourselves, and in some measure make up for all that has happened amiss.

And, lastly, holy joy is very pleasing to God. God delights in the joy of His creatures. He made them to be happy. His first and original design in the creation of all beings is His own glory in their happiness. When His people rejoice He rejoices. Some of you spent Christmas Day in the bosom of your families. Possibly you have a large family. Ten or twelve were at home on that day, with a grandchild or two. I will tell you what was your greatest joy on that day. It was to see the happiness of your children and to mark how they enjoyed what you had provided for them. They are only little children, some of them, creeping about on the floor, but they pleased you because they were so pleased themselves. The crow of a little child delights your heart to hear it, for it gives us joy to behold joy in those we love. Suppose your sons and daughters had all come marching in on Christmas Day in a very gloomy state of mind—cold, loveless, joyless. Suppose that they did not enjoy anything but grumbled at you and at one another, you would be quite sad and wish the day to be soon over and never come again for the next seven years. Thus, in a figure we see that our heavenly Father delights in the delight of His children and is glad to see them grateful and happy and acting as children should do toward such a Parent.

The Joy of the Lord

Alexander Maclaren (1826–1910) was one of Great Britain's most famous preachers. While pastoring the Union Chapel, Manchester (1858–1903), he became known as "the prince of expository preachers." Rarely active in denominational or civic affairs, Maclaren invested his time in studying the Word in the original languages and in sharing its truths with others in sermons that are still models of effective expository preaching. He published a number of books of sermons, and the climax of his ministry was publication of the monumental *Expositions of Holy Scripture*.

This message was taken from *Sermon Preached in Manchester,* first series, published by Funk and Wagnalls Company in 1902.

ALEXANDER MACLAREN

5

The Joy of the Lord

The joy of the LORD is your strength. (Nehemiah 8:10)

JUDAISM, IN ITS FORMAL AND CEREMONIAL ASPECT, was a religion of gladness. The feast was the great act of worship. It is not to be wondered at that Christianity, the perfecting of that ancient system, has been less markedly felt to be a religion of joy. It brings with it far deeper and more solemn views about man in his nature, condition, responsibilities, and destinies than ever prevailed before under any system of worship. And yet all deep religion ought to be joyful, and all strong religion assuredly will be.

Here, in the incident before us, there has come a time in Nehemiah's great enterprise when the Law, long forgotten, long broken by the captives, is now to be established again as the rule of the newly-founded commonwealth. Naturally enough there comes a remembrance of many sins in the past history of the people. Tears not unnaturally mingle with the thankfulness that again they are a nation, having a divine worship and a divine law in their midst. The leader of them, knowing for one thing that if the spirits of his people once began to flag that they could not face nor conquer the difficulties of their position, said to them, "This day is holy unto the LORD your

God; [this feast that we are keeping is a day of devout worship; therefore] mourn not, nor weep. . . . Go your way, eat the fat, and drink the sweet, and send portions unto them for whom nothing is prepared: . . . neither be ye sorry; for the joy of the LORD is your strength" (Neh. 8:9–10). You will make nothing of it by indulgence in lamentation and in mourning. You will have no more power for obedience. You will not be fit for your work if you fall into a desponding state. Be thankful and glad, and remember that the purest worship is the worship of God-fixed joy: "The joy of the LORD is your strength." And that is as true with regard to us as it ever was in these old times. We, I think, need the lesson contained in this saying of Nehemiah's because of some prevalent tendencies among us no less than these Jews did. Take some simple thoughts suggested by this text that are both important in themselves and needful to be made emphatic because so often forgotten in the ordinary type of Christian character. They are these. Religious joy is the natural result of faith. It is a Christian duty. It is an important element in Christian strength.

Joy Is the Natural Result of Christian Faith

First, joy in the Lord is the natural result of Christian faith. There is a natural adaptation or provision in the gospel, both by what it brings to us and by what it takes away from us to make a calm, settled, and deep gladness the prevalent temper of the Christian spirit. In what it gives us, I say, and in what it takes away from us. It gives us what we call well a sense of acceptance with God. It gives us God for the rest of our spirits. It gives us the communion with Him, which in proportion as it is real will be still. And in proportion as it is still will be all bright and joyful. It takes away from us the fear that lies before us, the strifes that lie within us, the desperate conflict that is waged between a man's conscience and his inclinations, between his will and his passions, which tears the heart asunder and always makes sorrow and tumult wherever it comes. It takes away the sense of sin. It gives us, instead of the torpid conscience or the angrily-stinging conscience, a conscience all calm from its accusations with all the sting drawn out of it. For quiet peace lies in the heart of the man that is trusting in the Lord. The gospel works joy, because the soul is at rest in God; joy, because every function of the spiritual nature has found now its haven and its object; joy, because health has come, and the healthy working of the body or of the spirit is itself a gladness; joy, because the dim future is painted (where it is painted at all) with shapes of light and beauty, and because the very vagueness of these is an element in the greatness of its revelation. The joy that is in Christ is deep and abiding. Faith in Him naturally works gladness.

I do not forget that, on the other side, it is equally true that the Christian faith has as marked and almost as strong an adaptation to produce a solemn *sorrow*—solemn, manly, noble, and strong. "As sorrowful, yet alway rejoicing" (2 Cor. 6:10), is the rule of the Christian life. If we think of what our faith does, of the light that it casts upon our condition, upon our nature, upon our responsibilities, upon our sins, and upon our destinies, we can easily see how, if gladness be one part of its operation, no less really and truly is sadness another. All great thoughts have a solemn quiet in them, which not infrequently merges into a still sorrow. There is nothing more contemptible in itself, and there is no more sure mark of a trivial nature and a trivial round of occupations than unshaded gladness that rests on no deep foundations of quiet, patient grief. Grief, because I know what I am and what I ought to be; grief, because I have learned the "exceeding sinfulness of sin"; grief, because, looking out upon the world, I see, as other men do not see, hell-fire burning at the back of the mirth and the laughter, and know what it is that men are hurrying to!

Do you remember who it was that stood by the side of the one poor dumb man whose tongue He was going to loose, and looking up to heaven *sighed* before He could say, "Be opened" (Mark 7:34)? Do you remember that of Him it is said, "God, hath anointed thee with the oil of gladness above thy fellows"

(Ps. 45:7; Heb. 1:9); also, "a man of sorrows, and acquainted with grief" (Isa. 53:3)? And do you not think that both these characteristics are to be repeated in the operations of His gospel upon every heart that receives it? And if, by the hopes it breathes into us, by the fears that it takes away from us, by the union with God that it accompanies for us, by the fellowship that it implants in us, it indeed anoints us all "with the oil of gladness." Yet, on the other hand, by the sense of mine own sin that it teaches me; by the conflict with weakness that it makes to be the law of my life; by the clear vision that it gives me of the "law in my members, warring against the law of my mind, and bringing me into captivity" (Rom. 7:23); by the intensity that it breathes into all my nature, and by the thoughts that it presents of what sin leads to and what the world at present is, the gospel, wherever it comes, will infuse a wise, valiant, sadness as the very foundation of character.

Yes, joy, but sorrow too! The joy of the Lord, but sorrow as we look on our own sin and the world's woe! The head anointed with the oil of gladness, but also crowned with thorns. These two are not contradictory. These two states of mind, both of them the natural operations of any deep faith, may coexist and blend into one another so as that the gladness is sobered, chastened, and made manly and noble. The sorrow is like some thundercloud, all streaked with bars of sunshine that go into its deepest depths. The joy lives in the midst of the sorrow. The sorrow springs from the same root as the gladness. The two do not clash against each other or reduce the emotion to a neutral indifference, but they blend into one another. Just as in the Arctic regions (deep down beneath the cold snow with its white desolation and its barren death), you shall find the budding of the early spring flowers and the fresh green grass. Just as some kinds of fire burn below the water; just as, in the midst of the barren and undrinkable sea, there may be welling up some little fountain of fresh water that comes from a deeper depth than the great ocean around it and pours its sweet streams along the surface of the salt waste.

Gladness, because I love, for love *is* gladness; gladness, because I trust, for trust *is* gladness; gladness, because I obey, for obedience is a "meat to eat that ye know not of" (John 4:32), and light comes when we do His will! But sorrow, because still I am wrestling with sin; sorrow, because still I have not perfect fellowship; sorrow, because mine eye, purified by my living with God, sees earth, sin, life, death, the generations of men, and the darkness beyond in some measure as God sees them! And yet, the sorrow is surface, and the joy is central. The sorrow springs from circumstance, and the gladness from the essence of the thing; therefore the sorrow is transitory, and the gladness is perennial. For the Christian life is all like one of those sweet spring showers in early April, when the raindrops weave for us a mist that hides the sunshine; and yet the hidden sun is in every sparkling drop. They are all saturated and steeped in its light. "The joy of the LORD" is the natural result and offspring of all Christian faith.

Joy Is a Matter of Christian Duty

And now, secondly, the "joy of the LORD," or rejoicing in God, is a matter of Christian duty. It is a commandment here, and it is a command in the New Testament as well. "Neither be ye sorry, for the joy of the LORD is your strength." I need not quote to you the frequent repetitions of the same injunction that the apostle Paul gives us: "Rejoice in the Lord alway: and again I say, Rejoice" (Phil. 4:4); "Rejoice evermore" (1 Thess. 5:16), and the like. The fact that this joy has enjoined us suggests to us a thought or two worth looking at.

You may say with truth, "My emotions of joy and sorrow are not under my own control. I cannot help being glad and sad as circumstances dictate. But yet here it lies, a commandment. It is a duty, a thing that the apostle enjoins. Of course, it follows that somehow or other it is to a large extent within one's own power. Even the indulgence in this emotion, and the degree to which a Christian life shall be a cheerful life, is dependent in a large measure on our own volitions and stands on the same footing as our obedience to God's other commandments.

We *can* to a very great extent control even our own emotions. But then, besides, we can do more than that. It may be quite true that you cannot help feeling sorrowful in the presence of sorrowful thoughts, and glad in the presence of thoughts that naturally kindle gladness. But I will tell you what you can do or refrain from doing. You can either go and stand in the light, or you can go and stand in the shadow. You can either fix your attention upon and make the predominant subject of your religious contemplations a truth, which shall make you glad and strong, or a half-truth, which shall make you sorrowful and, therefore, weak. Your meditations may either center mainly upon your own selves, your faults and failings, and the like; or they may center mainly upon God and His love, Christ and His grace, the Holy Spirit and His communion. You may either fill your soul with joyful thoughts or–though a true Christian, a real, devout, God-accepted believer–you may be so misapprehending the nature of the gospel and your relation to it, its promises and precepts, its duties and predictions as that the prevalent tinge and cast of your religion shall be solemn and almost gloomy. It is not lighted up and irradiated with the felt sense of God's presence–with the strong, healthy consciousness that you are a forgiven and a justified man, and that you are going to be a glorified one.

And thus far (and it is a long way), by the selection or the rejection of the appropriate and proper subjects that shall make the main portion of our religious contemplation and shall be the food of our devout thoughts, we *can* determine the complexion of our religious life. Just as you inject coloring matter into the fibers of some anatomical preparation, so a Christian may, as it were, inject into all the veins of his religious character and life either the bright tints of gladness or the dark ones of self-despondency. The result will be according to the thing that he has put into them. If your thoughts are chiefly occupied with God and what He has done and is for you, then you will have peaceful joy. If, on the other hand, they are bent ever on yourself and your own unbelief, then you will always be sad. You can make your choice.

The joy of the Lord is a duty, Christian people. It is so because, as we have seen, it is the natural effect of faith, because we can do much to regulate our emotions directly, and much more to determine them by determining what set of thoughts shall engage us. A wise and strong faith is our duty. To keep our emotional nature well under control of reason and will is our duty. To lose thoughts of ourselves in God's truth about Himself is our duty. If we do these things, we cannot fail to have Christ's joy remaining in us and making ours full. If we have not that blessed possession abiding with us, which He lived and died to give us, there is something wrong in us somewhere.

It seems to me that this is a truth which we have great need, my friends, to lay to heart. It is of no great consequence that we should practically confute the impotent, old sneer about religion as being a gloomy thing. One does not need to mind much what some people say on that matter. The world would call "the joy of the LORD" gloom, just as much as it calls "godly sorrow" gloom. But we are losing for ourselves a power and an energy of which we have no conception, unless we feel that joy is a duty. And unless we believe that not to be joyful in the Lord is, therefore, more than a misfortune, it is a fault.

I do not forget that the comparative absence of this happy, peaceful sense of acceptance, harmony, and oneness with God springs sometimes from temperament and depends on our natural dispositions. Of course the natural character determines to a large extent the perspective of our conceptions of Christian truth and the coloring of our inner religious life. I do not mean to say for a moment that there is one uniform type to which all must be conformed, or sin. There is indeed one type, the perfect manhood of Jesus, but it is all comprehensive. Each variety of our fragmentary manhood finds its own perfecting, and not its transmutation to another fashion of man, in being conformed to Him. Some of us are naturally fainthearted, timid, skeptical of any success, grave, melancholy, or hard to stir to any emotion. To such there will be an added difficulty in making quiet confident joy any very familiar guest in their home or in their place of prayer. But even such should remember that through the "powers of the world to come" (Heb. 6:5) the energies of the gospel are given to us for the very express purpose of overcoming as well as of hallowing natural dispositions. If it be our duty to rejoice in the Lord, it is no sufficient excuse to urge for not responding to the reiterated call, "In myself I am disposed to sadness."

While making all allowances for the diversities of character, which will always operate to diversify the history of the inner life in each individual, we think that in the great majority of instances there are two things, both faults, that have a great deal more to do with the absence of joy from much Christian experience than any unfortunate natural tendency to the dark side of things. The one is an actual deficiency in the depth and reality of our faith; the other is a misapprehension of the position that we have a right to take and are bound to take.

An actual deficiency in our faith. It is not to be wondered at that Christians do not find that the Lord with them is the Lord their strength and joy, as well as the Lord "their righteousness," when the amount of their fellowship with Him is so small and the depth of it so shallow as we usually find it. The first true vision that a sinful soul has of God, the imperfect beginnings of religion, usually are accompanied with intense self-abhorrence and sorrowing tears of penitence. A further closer vision of the love of God in Jesus Christ brings with it "joy and peace in believing" (Rom. 15:13). But the prolongation of these throughout life requires the steadfast continuousness of gaze toward Him. It is only where there is much faith and consequent love that there is much joy. Let us search our own hearts. If there is but little heat around the bulb of the thermometer, no wonder that the mercury marks a low degree. If there is but small faith, there will not be much gladness. The road into Giant Despair's castle is through doubt, which doubt comes from an absence, a sinful absence, in our own experience of the felt presence of God and the felt force of the verities of His gospel.

But then, besides that, there is another fault: not a fault in the sense of crime or sin, but a fault (and a great one) in the sense of error and misapprehension. We as Christians do not take the position that we have a right to take and that we are bound to take. Men venture themselves upon God's Word as they do on doubtful ice, timidly putting a light foot out to feel if it will bear them and always having the tacit fear, "Now, it is going to crack!" You must cast yourselves on God's gospel with all your weight, without any hanging back, without any doubt, without even the shadow of a suspicion that it will *give*—that the firm, pure floor will give and let you through into the water! A Christian shrinks from saying what the apostle said, "I *know* whom I have believed, and am persuaded that he is able to keep that which I have committed unto him against that day" (2 Tim. 1:12). A Christian fancies that salvation is a future thing and forgets that it is a present thing! A Christian trembles to profess "assurance of hope," forgetting that there is no hope strong enough to bear the stress of a life's sorrows that is not a conviction certain as one's own existence. Friends, understand that the gospel is a gospel that brings a present salvation and try to feel that it is not presumption, but simply acting out the very fundamental principle of it when you are not afraid to say, "I *know* that my Redeemer is yonder, and I *know* that He loves me!" Try to feel, I say, that by faith you have a right to take that position, "Now are we the sons of God" (1 John 3:2). Try to feel that you have a right to claim for yourselves, and that you are falling beneath the loftiness of the gift that is given to you unless you do claim for yourselves, the place of sons and daughters accepted, loved, sure to be glorified at God's right hand. Am I teaching presumption? Am I teaching carelessness or a dispensing with self-examination? No, but I am saying this: If a man has once felt, and feels in however small and feeble a degree, depressed by whatsoever sense of daily transgressions, if he feel faint like the first movement of an imprisoned bird in its egg, the feeble pulse of an almost imperceptible and imperceptible faith beat, then that man has a right to say, "God is mine!"

As one of our great teachers, not long gone from us, said, "Let me take my personal salvation for granted" . . . and what? and "be idle"? No! ". . . and *work* from it." Yes, a Christian is not to be forever asking himself, "Am I a Christian?" He is not to be forever looking into himself for marks and signs that he is. He *is* to look into himself to discover sins that he may by God's help cast them out, to discover sins that shall teach him to say with greater thankfulness, "What a redemption this is which I possess!" But he is to base his convictions that he is God's child upon something other than his own characteristics and the feebleness of his own strength. He is to have "joy in the LORD" (Isa. 29:19) whatever may be his sorrow from outward things. And I believe that if Christian people would lay that thought to heart, they would understand better how the natural operation of the gospel is to make gladness, and how rejoicing in the Lord is a Christian duty.

Joy Is a Source of Christian Strength

And now with regard to the other thought that still remains to be considered, namely, that rejoicing in the Lord is a source of strength. I have already anticipated, fragmentarily, nearly all that I could have said here in a more systematic form. All gladness has something to do with our efficiency; for it is the prerogative of man that his force comes from his mind and not from his body. That old song about a sad heart tiring in a mile is as true in regard to the gospel and the works of Christian people as in any other case. If we have hearts full of light and souls at rest in Christ, and the wealth and blessedness of a tranquil gladness lying there and filling our being, work will be easy, endurance will be easy, sorrow will be bearable, trials will not be so very hard. Above all temptations we shall be lifted and set upon a rock. If the soul is full, and full of joy, what side will be exposed to the assault of *any* temptation? If it appeal to fear, the gladness that is there is an answer. If it appeal to passion, desire, wish for pleasure of any sort, there is no need for any more—the heart is *full.* And so the gladness that rests in Christ will be a gladness that will fit us for all service and for all endurance, which will be unbroken by any sorrow. Like the magic shield of the old legends, invisible, slender, in its crystalline purity, will stand before the tempted heart and will repel all the "fiery darts of the wicked."

"The joy of the LORD is your strength," my friend. Nothing else is. No vehement resolutions, no sense of your own sinfulness, nor even contrite remembrance of past failures ever made a man strong yet. It made him weak that he might become strong, and when it had done that it had done its work. For strength there must be hope; for strength there must be joy. If the arm is to smite with vigor, it must smite at the bidding of a calm and light heart. The Christian work is of such a sort as that the most dangerous opponent to it is simple despondency and simple sorrow. "The joy of the LORD is strength."

Well then, there are two questions: How comes it that so much of the world's joy is weakness? And how comes it that so much of the world's notion of religion is gloom and sadness? Answer them for yourselves, and remember: You are weak unless you are glad. You are not glad and strong unless your faith and hope are fixed in Christ, and unless you are working from and not toward the assurance of salvation, from and not toward the sense of pardon, from and not toward the conviction of acceptance with God!

Joy and Peace in Believing

George H. Morrison (1866–1928) assisted the great Alexander Whyte in Edinburgh, pastored two churches, and then, in 1902, became pastor of the distinguished Wellington Church on University Avenue in Glasgow, Scotland. His preaching drew great crowds; in fact, people had to line up an hour before the services to ensure that they got seats in the large auditorium. Morrison was a master of imagination in preaching, yet his messages are solidly biblical.

From his many published volumes of sermons, I have chosen this message, found in *The Return of the Angels,* published in 1909 by Hodder and Stoughton, London.

6

Joy and Peace in Believing

Now the God of hope fill you with all joy and peace in believing.
(Romans 15:13)

It is a question that we ought seriously to ask ourselves, at the approach of a Communion season, if we are in possession of the joy and peace that form the benediction of our text. Can we truly say that we know in our own hearts what the apostle calls joy and peace in believing? Is this the deepest result of that religion which we profess and in which we have been bred? And is it so, not only on the Sabbath and under the calming influences of the sanctuary, but amid the cares, the worries, the distractions that await every worshiper tomorrow? In other words, *try* to suppose for a moment that your religion were withdrawn from you. Try to conceive yourself without your faith, though in every other particular unchanged. Then tell me, would you be appreciably the poorer, would you feel that any peace and joy had gone, would anyone detect that you were different and that some secret thing had passed away? When a loved one dies, the blindest eye can see that our gladness and our quiet are in eclipse. Now just suppose your religion were to die—would that be witnessed in a similar way? Such questions we ought to ask ourselves as we look forward to the Holy Sacrament.

Joy and Peace in Working

Contrast, for instance, joy and peace in believing with joy and peace in *working*. Most of us can say with perfect truth that we have experienced joy and peace in working. Not always, certainly, for sometimes work is wearisome, and sometimes it is ill-suited to our bent. And there are days, and sometimes there are years, when men are physically unfit for duty. But granting that, is it not the case that we have experienced joy and peace in working, and that if our work were taken away, much of our joy and peace would also go? Of working, we can say that in sincerity. What I want to ask is, can we say it of believing? Is there anything in our religious life that answers to that feature in our active life? I put that question to you very seriously as you look forward to the bread and wine. Honestly and as between yourself and God, have you joy and peace in believing?

Joy and Peace in Loving

Or think again of joy and peace in *loving*. There are few who have not had experience of that. "Perfect love casteth out fear: because fear hath torment" (1 John 4:18). Think, for example, of the Christian home, that beautiful creation of the gospel. Imperfect though it must necessarily be, is it not the dwelling place of joy and peace? And all the joy of it and all the peace, which are deeper and truer than any passing shadow, rest on and are continually refreshed by the presence in the Christian home of love. Deeper than all rebellion of the child is the child's love for father and for mother. Mightier than any care or worry is the love of the mother for her children. And that is the secret of the Christian home, however poorly it be realized. It is the sphere above all other spheres where there is joy and peace in loving.

Now Paul does not speak of joy and peace in loving. He speaks of joy and peace in believing. And the one we know. We have experienced it. It has been ours in childhood and in manhood. But the question is, what about the other? Have we known anything of it at all? Do we go up and down the world with a glad peace because we believe in God through Jesus Christ? It is to that that we are called, whatever our temperament or our lot. The gospel is good news. It is the gladdest news that ever broke upon the heart of man. It is not given to bow us to the ground with a burden too heavy to be borne. It is here amid all the ills that we are heir to, to make us more than conquerors in Christ. Now I ask you, as you look forward to Communion, has it had that effect on you? Amid your worries and sicknesses and sorrows, have you had joy and peace just in believing? And if not, I want to ask why not? Why have you missed the strengthening of it all? When God is offering, why have you never taken the very blessing that you sorely need.

Think for a moment of the kind of people to whom these words were originally sent. They were sent to a little company of Christians whose lot was very far from being easy. Separated from us by well nigh two thousand years, we are prone to think of them as dim and shadowy. If our own woes grow dim with passing years, how much more those of centuries ago. Yet they had sorrows as intense as ours, and trials that were very dark and bitter. They had hearts that were as full of sin as any that are throbbing here today. They were called to be saints, and yet they were not saints. They were just poor and faulty men and women. And some were slaves, and some were city merchants, and some were mothers in undistinguished homes. Yet Paul, when he thought of them, made no exceptions. Not one of them was excluded from the blessing. And not one of us within this church today is excluded from the blessing either. Am I speaking to any whose lot is hard and who scarce know how they can stand it longer? Am I speaking to any who have the sorrow's crown of sorrow in remembering happier things? Am I speaking to any for whom the way is desert, who are weary, who are disappointed? Am I speaking to any in such heaviness of grief that they doubt if the sun will ever shine again? If all we had to preach was resignation, then we might close the Bible and have done with preaching. For you do not need to come into the sanctuary to hear the ministry of resignation. But it is not that which is the gospel news–it is this, that there is joy and peace, a joy that is deeper than the deepest wound and a peace that the world cannot take away. Now, as a simple matter of experience have you found joy and peace in your religion? Ask yourself that. Be honest with yourself. Put it seriously to yourself today. You know what joy and peace in working are. You know what joy and peace in loving are. But joy and peace in believing, what of that? Lord, I believe, help thou mine unbelief.

Lest one should mistake the frame of mind which is here indicated as our peculiar privilege, observe how here, as elsewhere in the Scripture, joy and peace are linked together. There is a joy that has no peace in it. It is tumultuous, feverish, unsettled. It is too eager to be the friend of rest, too wild to have any kinship with repose. Its true companionship is with excitement. Like other passions it grows by what it feeds on, demanding ever a more powerful stimulus and in the end demanding it in vain. And then there is a peace that has no joy. It has no gladness in it whatsoever. It is like a dull and sluggish stream, moving in an uninteresting land. And there is nothing bright and beautiful around; no profusion of flowers on its banks; no vistas suddenly opening to the eye of depth of forest or majesty of hill. There is a joy that is devoid of peace. Such joy may burn–it never blesses. There is a peace that is devoid of joy. But not such is the peace of God.

Now the notable thing is that on the page of Scripture joy and peace are in the closest union. Wherever we light upon the one, we are not long in coming on the other. We sometimes say of inseparable friends that when you find the one you find the other. United in a comradeship of hearts, the one will not long be absent from the other. And so, remember, it is with joy and peace. As joy and peace move on the page of Scripture, the two are linked in a most holy wedlock, and "what . . . God hath joined together, let not man put asunder" (Matt. 19:6). "Peace I leave with you," said Jesus (John 14:27). Then, "these things have I spoken unto you . . . that your joy might be full" (15:11). "The kingdom of God is not meat and drink; but righteousness, and peace, and joy in the Holy Ghost" (Rom. 14:17). And the fruit of the Spirit is not love and joy. Paul does not stop his enumeration there. "The fruit of the Spirit is love, joy, peace" (Gal. 5:22). That then is the peculiar frame and the characteristic temper of the Christian—a joy that at the heart of it has peace, a peace that is so deep that it is glad. And yet how few of us can say today that the Spirit has inwrought that frame in us; how few possess what is for every one of us—joy and peace in believing.

Sometimes it may be we lack this inward comfort because we have lost the wonder of salvation. We are so familiar with the gospel message that we have ceased to feel the wonder of it all. Oh, if we only realized today the unspeakable wonder of the love of God, there is not one of us so hard and worldly but would be visited by joy and peace. And if we are not so visited, may not the reason be that we have heard of the love of God a thousand times, and we have grown so familiar with it all that it has little power to move us now. It is not the man who dwells amid the woods who feels most deeply their ministry of peace. It is not the children of unbroken sunshine who best appreciate the joy of sunshine. And it may be that dwelling with the gospel, as you and I have done since we were children, we have lost a little of the wonder of it all and made it less a thing of joy and peace.

Now I want to say to you that the Lord's Supper is exquisitely adapted for that state. You get nothing at the Table of the Lord that you do not get in the preaching of the gospel. But you get it pictorially and sacramentally. It is not spoken; it is seen and handled. That is why it is so powerful to quicken believing into joy and peace. Who can look upon the broken bread without seeing again the body that was broken? And Christ comes near to us, and He is living and dying for your sins and mine. Until touched afresh by the wonder of it all after the hardening of many days, our love is kindled, our faith begins to glow, and we feel the blessedness of joy and peace.

Sometimes, too, we fail in joy and peace because we meddle with things that are too high for us. We vex ourselves, and vex ourselves in vain, over the hidden things of the Almighty. It may be that there is something in our life that is very difficult to understand. Or we look abroad on evil in the city, and we say, Can God be witness to it all? Or the fate of the heathen weighs upon the heart, or the final state of those who have been Christless, or one or other of those mighty problems that are never far away from human thought. Now far be it from me to suggest that a Christian should never think upon these things. So constituted is the human mind that to think upon them is inevitable. But this I most emphatically say, that if in thinking so we lose our joy and peace, we are not trusting as we ought to trust and not living as we ought to live. It is our duty to cast our burden on the Lord, and the burden of many today is intellectual. It is our duty to honor Jesus Christ, if we would not have Him be ashamed of us. And we honor Him when amid all the darkness we believe that all is well for He is King. We honor Him not with a darkened heart, but with a believing full of joy and peace. If you were traveling in an ocean vessel when there fell on it a terrific storm, do you think the captain would feel honored in you if you worried him in an agony of fear? I shall tell you how he would be honored—by your continuing to be cheerful and at peace, and so continuing because you trusted him although the heavens were as black as pitch. It is thus, too, that we honor Jesus Christ. We honor Him by our joy and by our peace. The night is dark and we are far from home, but we are certain He is in command. And so we serve Him and help our brother. For His sake we do the little we can do, and there we leave it until the morning comes.

In closing let me point out to you, what in some degree is familiar to us all, how eminently fitted is the gospel message to create this inward frame of joy and peace. The gospel has not been given to make us sad. The gospel has been given to make us glad. It is good news—the gladdest of all news—the most glorious message the world has ever heard. O what a fool that man is who rejects it, as if it were a harsh and gloomy thing. It is the gladdest and most glorious news that was ever flashed upon the ear of man. Sweet is the message of the morning sun when it touches the window after a night of pain. Sweet is the message of returning spring when the time of the singing of birds is come again. But a thousand times sweeter, a thousand times more wonderful is that message as old as spring and yet as new—the message that has been ours since we were children and that shall be ours when the last shadows fall. Think of it—God is love. You can lift up your heart today and say, God loves me. Think of it—all your sins are pardoned and washed away in the blood of Jesus Christ. Think of it—you are the object of God's care, and He will never leave you nor forsake you. Neither death nor hell can ever touch you, for you are His and He is yours forever. Is that the kind of news to make one gloomy? Is that the kind of news to make one miserable? I tell you that if you only realized it you would rise up in your place and shout for joy. God help us all to realize it better—to feel the wonder and glory of it more until each of us rises with the Lord Jesus Christ into the experience of joy and peace!

Rest for Weary Feet

John Henry Jowett (1864–1923) was born in Yorkshire, England, and was known as "the greatest preacher in the English-speaking world." He was ordained into the Congregational ministry, and his second pastorate was at the famous Carr's Lane Church, Birmingham, where he followed the eminent Dr. Robert W. Dale. From 1911 to 1918, he pastored the Fifth Avenue Presbyterian Church, New York City; from 1918 to 1923, he ministered at Westminster Chapel, London, succeeding G. Campbell Morgan. He wrote many books of devotional messages and sermons.

This message was taken from *Apostolic Optimism,* published by Richard R. Smith, Inc., New York, in 1930.

7

Rest for Weary Feet

I will give you rest. (Matthew 11:28)

One of the youngest of our poets, and in many ways perhaps the most brilliant of them, William Watson, has given us some beautiful verses that were born in his soul as he stood by Wordsworth's grave. He asks himself what it was in Wordsworth that made him the sought companion of multitudes and that gave the poet a place among the immortals. He compares him with many others of our poets and finds that the excellent glories in which they shone he conspicuously lacks. He has none of "Milton's keen translucent music," none of " Shakespeare's cloudless, boundless human view." He has none of "Byron's tempest anger, tempest mirth." He lacks "the wizard twilight Coleridge knew," and "Shelley's flush of rose on peaks divine." In all these great poetic treasures, which his peers possess, Wordsworth is wanting. What endowment then had he of his own which could make amends for all this lack? Our poet answers, "He had, for weary feet, the gift of rest." That is Wordsworth's wealth–"for weary feet, the gift of rest." His poetry takes the heart, and just bathes and steeps it in an atmosphere of deep quietness and peace. He takes us away from the strife of tongues and from the hard and jarring noise of city life. He takes us away to that quiet land of lakes, on to those still uplands, whose only sounds are the cry of the peewit and the bleating of a wandering sheep. And as you read the poetry and feed upon its spirit, the stillness of the moorland and the mountain tarn enters in and pervades your soul, and you enjoy a sense of the most refreshing peace. He has "for weary feet, the gift of rest."

Yes, but put down your Wordsworth, and you are back again in the old city. You awake to the hard reality and noise of things, and the still atmosphere of the poem has gone like the fabric of a dream. The old world is as clamorous as ever. Its ways are as rough and stony as ever. Its rude and thoughtless jostlings are as painful and as breathless as ever. Your feet are soon again weary, and your heart is tired and sore. The poet's gift of rest is beautiful and not to be despised. It provides a short holiday for the soul, but only a holiday. It is only a temporary respite from which it must return to the old monotonous beaten ways and soon finds itself wearied with the old strife, the old care, the old sin. But the soul craves not merely for a holiday, a temporary tent life on some poetic hill, but for "a rest that remaineth" (see Heb. 4:9)–to use the apostolic word–even when we are in the midst of strife and trouble and death. That is the rest for which the weary heart craves and which no poet has it in his power to give. His gift of rest is a holiday; we want the rest of the Eternal, the changeless rest.

But there is Another who claims to have for weary feet the gift of rest. The world is always full of weary feet, and the days of the Nazarene were no exception. The souls that gathered about Him numbered a great many weary ones–tired, self-nauseated, faint. He looked upon them, saw their weariness, and was moved with infinite pity. He thus appealed to them: "Come unto me all ye that labour and are heavy laden, and I will give you rest" (Matt. 11:28). "I will give." How? You remember that other great word He spoke on another day: "Not as the world giveth, give I" (John 14:27). How does the world give? If the world wished to help a heavy-laden man, it would seek to do it by removing his burden. The world's way of giving rest is by removing a man's yoke. "Not as the world giveth, give I." The world would create a paradise of sluggards. The world's heaven would be a life without burdens. Its gift of rest would be a gift of ease. "Not as the world giveth, give I." That is not His way. The restful life is not the easeful life–life without burdens or yokes. The gift of Jesus is a gift of rest while wearing the yoke, rest while carrying the cross, rest in the very midst of mystery, temptation, and strife. "Come unto me, all ye that labour and are heavy laden, and I will give you rest."

Now, let us look at one or two types of weary feet to which this Savior will, with infinite gladness, bring the gift of rest. Look around you. Where would you look to find the most weary feet in the city? Where would you find the soul most tired and wearied? You would not necessarily find it in homes that had been the scenes of great and burdensome sorrow. The deepest weariness is not the accompaniment of the deepest grief. Through the darkest sorrows the soul can often "walk, and not faint" (Isa. 40:31), so that I don't think I should seek out the homes of blackest sorrow if I wished to find the most weary life. Where then should we find it? Look at those twelve disciples who were chosen by our Lord. Which of them would you think experienced the deepest weariness of spirit? Would you single out Thomas and say that his very proneness to doubt must have often filled him with deep weariness as he encountered so much that was mysterious and perplexing? Or would you point out John and say that his clear vision of the ideal life, with all its love and light and truth, must have created a deep sense of weariness as he compared the ideal with the real and saw how unfriendly the world was to the pure and the true? Or would you pick out Peter and say that a man who was always resolving and always failing must have often sunk into a profound weariness, and felt as though it were useless for his tired and beaten soul to strive any more? I think that each of these disciples must have known at times a really deep weariness of spirit, and yet I would have chosen none of these if I wanted to select the man who experienced the most terrible weariness of all. I should have put my hand upon Judas Iscariot. I should say that he knew seasons of weariness of which the apostle John could not conceive. And why? Because he was a selfish man, the most selfish heart in the disciple band.

There is no weariness like the weariness that gathers around a selfish heart. If we could place our finger upon the most selfish heart in the city, we should have discovered a life that moves with terribly weary feet. Why, such a character is a commonplace in fiction because it is a commonplace in life. Think of any selfish character in fiction whom you can call to mind, and you will find that he moves through discontentments and dissatisfactions and continued unrest. A man who lives entirely for himself becomes at last obnoxious to himself. I believe it is the very law of God that self-centeredness ends in self-nauseousness. There is no weariness like the weariness of a man who is wearied of himself, and that is the awful Nemesis that follows the selfish life. I am inclined to believe that a great deal of the tiredness and weariness of the world, perhaps more than we commonly think, is only the sickly loathing and self-disgust arising from a morbid selfishness, however much we may strive to attribute it to something else. Be that as it may, there is one truth that may be proclaimed with absolute dogmatism, that selfishness inevitably tends to create self-nausea and weary feet.

Well, you know what remedy we commonly prescribe for such complaints. What do we say of the selfish man who is weary, discontented, full of jadedness and unrest? What do his fellows say of him? They say, "He wants to get away from himself." It is a very suggestive phrase. A man getting away from *himself!* For why? For *rest!* If he could only get away from himself, he would lose that sense of weariness and nausea and find a pleasing rest. It is only another way of expressing the truth, which is so beautifully worded in one of the hymns we sing, where we pray for "a heart at leisure from itself." "A heart at leisure from itself!"—a heart that gets away from itself, that does not stay brooding over itself, fondling itself, nursing itself, until it loathes itself in weariness—and by its absence from itself finding strength and rest.

Now, listen to the Master: "Come unto me, [ye weary, selfish ones], and I will give you rest." And how will He do it? By taking us away from ourselves, by giving us leisure from ourselves, by making us unselfish. When a weary, selfish heart comes to the Savior, the Savior meets his need by saying, "Take my yoke upon you." "But, Lord, he is tired and weary already. Another yoke will crush him." No, no! He has just been carrying himself, and himself only, and that is the heaviest of all loads, heavier than any man can bear. But strange as it is, if he adds another burden, his own burden will become light. That is the mystery of grace, that the burdens of a selfish man are lightened by adding more. "Take my yoke upon you." And what yoke is that, Lord? The yoke of other people's needs, the burdens of the blind and the deaf and the lame and the lepers, the burdens of other folk's sorrows. Put them onto your shoulders—"take my yoke upon you"—increase your burden, and your burden shall become light, and instead of weariness you shall find rest. Now, it may be that there are weary hearts among my hearers whose weariness is only the measure of their selfishness, and for them this old word is true. Jesus will give you rest by giving you His yoke; He will add to your burden and so make your burden light. He will enlarge your thought to take in others and so give you leisure from yourselves. He will take away your jadedness and give you His own rest. You "shall run, and not be weary," you shall "walk, and not faint" (Isa. 40:31).

But selfishness, while it accounts for much, does not explain all the weariness of the world. The weariness of selfishness can be expelled by unselfish Christian service. But the unselfish often have weary feet and crave the gift of rest. Can this Savior meet the need? Let us look around us. What kind of weary lives do we see? There are the anxious ones. The Master could see many of them in the crowd to whom He was speaking—anxious ones living in fear of the unknown, unable to rest upon today, however bright and fair it be, because today so speedily changes into tomorrow, and tomorrow is all unknown. It is this great surrounding unknown that creates our anxiety and feeds it into strength. That dark unknown is the parent of our fears. Well, this anxiety, this continued tension of spirit, produces great spiritual exhaustion. The anxious soul moves with weary feet and would fain meet with one who had the gift of rest. I say our Master saw these anxious ones among His hearers and to them He cried, "Come unto me, ye . . . heavy laden [ones], and I will give you rest."

How does He give it? I want you to notice the verses that immediately precedes the words that I have quoted. I am afraid we sometimes ignore them because of the magnificence of the promise that follows. But they seem to me to have a very close and vital connection with the promise itself. The Master saw how many souls there were who were troubled and anxious about the unknown. And *He* knew the great secret which, if accepted, would set all their hearts at rest. What did He know? He knew God! If everybody knew God, nobody would be anxious. He knew Him and would unveil Him. "Neither knoweth any man the Father, save the Son, and he to whomsoever the Son will reveal him" (Matt. 11:27). "Come unto me, [ye anxious, laden ones], and I will give you rest." To you shall that dark unknown be filled with the Father's face, and your anxiety shall be changed into assurance and peace.

Have I succeeded in making the connection between these verses plain? The Savior seems to say, "If they only knew their Father, their anxiety would vanish like cloud spots in the dawn. I know the Father; I will make Him known to them. "Come unto Me, you anxious ones, and by a wondrous revelation I will give you rest." And so He seeks to turn weariness into rest by the unveiling of the Father. And in what strangely beautiful ways He made the Father known! He told them that to Providence there were no trifles, that God did not merely control great things and allow smaller things to go by chance. "The very hairs of your head are all numbered" (Matt. 10:30; Luke 12:7). Nothing is overlooked; all is full of thought and purpose.

"Look at that sparrow," He said, "how very lightly you regard it: a cheap thing: two of them sold for a farthing: and yet your Father *knows* when a sparrow falls! Be not anxious! God is thinking about all things! If the world were moving irrationally, without controlling thought, then anxiety would be natural and pardonable. But all things are happening in the thought of God, and God is love" (see Matt. 10:29–31).

That was the revelation the Savior made. Will anyone say that if accepted it would not end the anxiety of the world and turn its weariness of mind into rest? To come to Jesus is to take His revelation of the Father and to live in the inspiration of it. Such inspiration would turn fear into confidence and confidence into peace. Think of it. Suppose that the sky of our souls instead of being an "unknown," which might prove treacherous, were a Father's face, gracious and beneficent, and suppose that we lived in "the light of thy countenance" (Ps. 89:15), and never lost sight of it for a day, don't you think that that would create within us confidence out of which would spring eternal rest? The apostle Paul accepted the revelation of Jesus and lived in it and through it, and when dark days came he quietly sang, "I know whom I have believed, and am persuaded that he is able" (2 Tim. 1:12). That was just what the Master said, "If only they knew Him, their anxiety would change into an untroubled peace." And here is Paul confirming the Master's word: "I *know* whom I have believed, and am persuaded that he is able." And in the days of darkness and persecution he remained steadfast and unmovable, enjoying the very rest of God. "Come unto me, all ye weary, anxious ones, and I will reveal to you your Father, and in the beauty of the revelation ye shall discover the gift of rest."

The Virtue of Forbearance

George H. Morrison (1866–1928) assisted the great Alexander Whyte in Edinburgh, pastored two churches, and then, in 1902, became pastor of the distinguished Wellington Church on University Avenue in Glasgow, Scotland. His preaching drew great crowds; in fact, people had to line up an hour before the services to ensure that they got seats in the large auditorium. Morrison was a master of imagination in preaching, yet his messages are solidly biblical.

From his many published volumes of sermons, I have chosen this message found in *The Unlighted Lustre,* published in 1909 by Hodder and Stoughton, London.

8

The Virtue of Forbearance

Forbearing one another. (Colossians 3:13)

IF A MAN IS TO LIVE WITH ANY JOY AND FULLNESS, and to find what a noble abode this world may prove, there are three virtues that he must steadily pursue. The first is faith in God, for without faith existence will always be a tangled skein; the second is courage, for every life has its hills and we ascend them but poorly if our heart is faint; the third is forbearance–forbearing one another. It is on forbearance, then, that I desire to speak, and I propose to gather up what I wish to say in this way. First, I shall touch on some of the evils of the unforbearing spirit. Second, I shall indicate the character of true forbearance. Then I shall suggest some thoughts to make us more forbearing.

Evils of the Unforbearing Spirit

First, then, some of the evils of the unforbearing spirit. One of the first of them to arrest me is that it makes life a constant disappointment. I have often wondered that there is no trace of disappointment in the life of our Lord Jesus Christ. You may call Him a despised man if you will, but you could never call Him a disappointed man. "He came unto his own, and his own received him not" (John 1:11). They laughed Him to scorn and then they crucified Him. Yet when He entered the glory and saw His Father's face, do you think He said, "Father, it has been a tragic disappointment?" For all its sorrow, life was not *that* to Christ. It was full and fresh and dew-touched to the close, and one of the sources of that unfailing freshness was our Savior's knowledge of the secret of forbearance. Jesus expected great things from humanity. Jesus never expected the impossible. I like to think that He who made the heavens was ready when the hour came to make allowances. Depend upon it that if we expect the impossible we are doomed to the disappointment that is worse than death. There is only one highway to the world's true comradeship–it is the road of forbearing one another.

Another evil of the unforbearing spirit is this, that it presses hardest on life's most tender relationships. It becomes powerful for evil in that very region where ties are most delicate and life most sweet. There are some worms that are content to gnaw green leaves and to spend their lives on the branches of the tree. But there are others that are never satisfied with leaves, they must eat their way into the red heart of the rose. That is the curse of the unforbearing spirit–it gnaws at the very heart of the rose of life. It is comparatively easy to be forbearing with those whom we rarely meet and whom we hardly know. We are all tolerant of those who lightly touch us. But it is with those whom we meet and among whom we mingle daily who share the same home with us, who live with us and love us that it is often hardest to forbear, and it is on those that the sorrow of unforbearance falls. There are ministers who can speak well of every congregation, except the one that they have been called to serve. There are husbands who are gentle to everybody's faults, excepting to the faults of their own wives. And it is just because unforbearance has a greater scope in proportion as life's ties grow more tender and dear that the gospel of love insists so urgently on the duty of forbearing one another.

But there is another evil of the unforbearing temper. It reacts with certainty upon the man himself. "For with what judgment ye judge, ye shall be judged: and with what measure ye mete, it shall be measured to you again" (Matt. 7:2). If we are intolerant, we become intolerable. If we never make allowances for anybody, God knows the scant allowance that we get. Just think of the Pharisees a moment. Their crowning vice was that they were unforbearing. There was not a little that was good in many Pharisees, but they were harsh and censorious and exacting. Need I remind you of the vials of stern judgment that were poured on the Pharisees by Jesus Christ? Let that suffice for the evils of unforbearance. It makes life one constant disappointment. It presses hardest on life's most tender ties. It reacts inevitably on the man himself.

The Character of True Forbearance

In the second place, I wish to indicate the character of true forbearance, and it is urgently important that we should pay heed to this. For the Devil has gotten his counterfeit of every grace, and a counterfeit grace is sometimes worse than sin.

The first thing that I would say about it is that true forbearance begins in a man's thought. It is a good thing to be forbearing in our acts, a great thing to be so in our speech, yet I question if we have begun to practice rightly this preeminently Christian virtue until we are habitually forbearing in our thoughts. "Master," said the disciples, "shall we call down fire on these villages? They would not receive us. Shall we clear them away like Sodom?" (see Luke 9:54). And it was not quite for their *words* that Christ rebuked them–"ye know not what manner of *spirit* ye are of" (v. 55). Ah! if our bitter and unforbearing words flashed into utterance without any thought, they would not wound so, nor would they leave these scars that the kindnesses of weeks cannot efface. It is because they so often betray the unforbearing thoughts that have been harbored in secret and cherished in the dark that the bite of them is like a serpent's tooth. We talk of a hasty word, but a hasty word might mean little if it were only the out flash of a hasty thought. What a hasty word often implies is this: that in secret we have been putting the worst construction upon things, then comes the moment of temper when the tongue is loosened. We never meant to utter what we thought, but it escapes us—only a hasty word—yet the bitter thoughts of a fortnight may be in it. True forbearance begins in a man's thought.

Again true forbearance is independent of our moods. It does not vary with our varying temper. It is a mock forbearance that comes and goes with every variation in the day. There are times when it is very easy to be forbearing. When things have gone well with us, when we are feeling strong, or when some great happiness has touched our hearts, it is not difficult to be forbearing then. When we are in a good humor with ourselves, we can be in a good humor with everybody. But true forbearance is not a passing gleam, nor is it the child of a happy mood or temper. It does not depend on the state of a man's health, or on whether or not he has had a good day at business. It is a virtue to be loyally practiced for Christ's sake whatever our mood or disappointment be. I should not have wondered much if Christ had been forbearing when He rode in triumph into Jerusalem. Amid the cries of Hosanna and the strewing of the palm branches it might have been easy to take kindly views. But when His face was marred more than any man's, when they were looking on Him whom they had pierced, when the nails were torture and when the cross was agony, was it not supremely hard to be forbearing then? Yet it was then that the Redeemer prayed, "Father, forgive them; for they know not what they do" (Luke 23:34). Forbearance must not vanish when we suffer.

There is one other mark on which I would insist, and it is this, that true forbearance helps to better things. It is like the sunshine which brings the summer nearer; it is part of that gentleness that makes men great. There is a certain lenient indulgence that is the very antipodes of this great virtue. There is a soft and easy way of smiling at all sin that may send a man to the Devil double speed. Such leniency is the leniency of the Antichrist. Christian forbearance never makes light of sin. It never oils the wheels of Satan's chariot. It can be stern; it whets its littering sword. If a man is a scoundrel, it can tell him so. But it never despairs, never passes final judgments, sees possibilities, touches the chord of brotherhood, until a man feels that someone believes in him, and sometimes it is heaven to feel that. One day they dragged a poor woman before Christ, and the Jews would have stoned her for she was taken in sin. But Jesus said, "Neither do I condemn thee: go and sin no more" (John 8:11), and I am certain she never so sinned again. Peter was saved by the forbearance of Christ Jesus: "And the Lord turned, and looked upon Peter" (Luke 22:61). Thomas was saved by the forbearance of Christ Jesus: "Reach hither thy hand, . . . and be not faithless, but believing" (John 20:27). The forbearance of Christ was a great moral power, and all Christian forbearance must share the same prerogative.

Thoughts to Help Make Us More Forbearing

Then, lastly, let me suggest some thoughts that may help to make us more forbearing.

First think how little we know of one another. We know far too little to be censorious or harsh. One secret of the perfect gentleness of Christ is His perfect knowledge of everyone He met. I suppose that most of us have known some man whom for years, perhaps, we used to judge unkindly. We never liked him and our thoughts of him were bitter. Then one day we learned the story of his life, and we found that long ago when the heavens were blue above him, there had fallen on his life some crushing blow. We say, "Ah! if we had only known that story, we should never have judged the man as we have done." It is well to remember how ignorant we are when we are tempted to be unforbearing. There may have been something in the upbringing that would explain a score of things if we but knew it. There may have been elements that made the temptation awful, yet how we jested and sneered when someone fell! Forbearing one another–because of life's complexity, because we cannot see, because we do not know, because only God can tell the million threads that are woven into the tapestry of being. Our very dearest are such strangers to us that it is always wisest to forbear.

Next think how greatly we ourselves need forbearance. Even if we do not give it, we all want it. I suppose we all irritate and alienate other people a thousand times more often than we ever dream of. If other people are doing so to us, it is but reasonable to think we are doing so to them. Never a sun sets but a man feels how easily he might have been misjudged that day. Never a morning breaks but a man knows that he will make demands on the forbearance of the world. We need forbearance, then let us give forbearance. We need to be kindly judged, then let us judge so. Let us forbear one another because of our own great need.

Lastly think how God has forborne us. The forbearance of God is a perpetual wonder. He has been willing that men should taunt Him with being idle, and He has been willing that men should say He did not care, rather than that He should seem an unforbearing God. Is there no secret passage in your life which being trumpeted abroad would quite have ruined you? God in His mercy has never blown that trumpet blast, and His longsuffering has been your salvation. Then we are such poor scholars in His school. We are so backward and so soon turned aside. We make so little progress in His teaching and are so keen about everything save Him–surely there is no forbearance in the world like the forbearance of our heavenly Father. It is a great example. Shall we not copy it? We can start again at home this very night. Days will be golden and silenced birds will sing when we revive the grace of forbearing one another.

NOTES

On Patience

John Wesley (1703–1781), with his brother Charles and with George Whitefield, founded the Methodist movement in Britain and America. On May 24, 1738, he had his great spiritual experience in a meeting at Aldersgate Street, when his "heart was strangely warmed" and he received assurance of salvation. Encouraged by Whitefield to do open-air preaching, Wesley soon was addressing thousands in spite of the fact that many churches were closed to him. The Methodist societies he formed became local churches that conserved the results of his evangelism. He wrote many books and preached forty thousand sermons during his long ministry.

This sermon was taken from *The Works of John Wesley,* volume 6, published by Baker in 1986. The set was originally published in 1872 by the Wesleyan Methodist Book Room, London.

9

On Patience

Let patience have her perfect work, that ye may be perfect and entire, wanting nothing. (James 1:4)

"MY BRETHREN," SAYS THE APOSTLE IN A PRECEDING VERSE, "count it all joy when ye fall into divers temptations" (James 1:2). At first view, this may appear a strange direction, seeing most temptations are "for the present . . . [not] joyous, but grievous" (Heb. 12:11). Nevertheless, you know by your own experience that "the trying of your faith worketh patience" (James 1:3). And if "patience have her perfect work, . . . ye [shall] be perfect and entire, wanting nothing."

It is not to any particular person or church that the apostle gives this instruction, but to all who are partakers of like precious faith and are seeking after that common salvation. For as long as any of us are upon earth, we are in the region of temptation. He who came into the world to save His people from their sins did not come to save them from temptation. He Himself "knew no sin" (2 Cor. 5:21). Yet, while He was in this vale of tears, "he . . . suffered being tempted" (Heb. 2:18). Herein He also left "us an example, that ye should follow his steps" (1 Peter 2:21). We are liable to a thousand temptations from the corruptible body variously affecting the soul. The soul itself, encompassed as it is with infirmities, exposes us to ten thousand more. And how many are the temptations that we meet with even from the good men (such, at least, they are in part in their general character) with whom we are called to converse from day to day! Yet what are these to the temptations we may expect to meet with from an evil world, seeing we all, in effect, dwell with Mesech, and have our habitation in the tents of Kedar (see Ps. 120:5)? Add to this, that the most dangerous of our enemies are not those that assault us openly. No!

> Angels our march oppose,
> Who still in strength excel:
> Our secret, sworn, eternal foes,
> Countless, invisible!

For is not our "adversary the devil, as a roaring lion" (1 Peter 5:8) with all his infernal legions still going "about seeking whom he may devour" (v. 8)? This is the case with all the children of men. Yes, and with all the children of God as long as they sojourn in this strange land. Therefore, if we do not willfully and carelessly rush into them, yet we shall surely "fall into divers temptations." Temptations innumerable as the stars of heaven, and those varied and complicated a thousand ways. But, instead of counting this a loss, as unbelievers would do, "count it all joy; . . . knowing . . . that the trying of your faith" (James 1:2–3), even when it is "tried with fire" (1 Peter 1:7), "worketh patience." But "let patience have her perfect work, that ye may be perfect and entire, wanting nothing."

But what is *patience?* We do not now speak of a heathen virtue, neither of a natural indolence, but of a gracious temper wrought in the heart of a believer by the power of the Holy Spirit. It is a disposition to suffer whatever pleases God in the manner and for the time that pleases Him. We, thereby, hold the middle way, neither ολιγωραντες, *despising* our sufferings, *making little* of them, passing over them lightly as if they were owing to chance or second causes, nor, on the other hand, εκλυομενοι, *affected too much, unnerved, dissolved, sinking under them.* We may observe that the proper object of patience is suffering, either in body or mind. Patience does not imply the not *feeling* this. It is not apathy or insensibility. It is at the utmost distance from stoical stupidity. Yes, it is at an equal distance from fretfulness or dejection. The patient believer is preserved from falling into either of these extremes by considering who is the Author of all his suffering. Even God his Father. What is the *motive* of His *giving us* to suffer? Not so properly His justice as His love. What is the *end* of it? "Our profit, that we might be partakers of his holiness" (Heb. 12:10).

Very nearly related to patience is *meekness,* if it be not rather a species of it. For may it not be defined patience of injuries, particularly affronts, reproach, or unjust censure? This teaches not to return evil for evil, or railing for railing, but contrariwise blessing. Our blessed Lord Himself seems to place a peculiar value upon this temper. This He peculiarly calls us to learn of Him, if we would find rest for our souls.

But what may we understand by the *work of patience?* "Let patience have her perfect work." It seems to mean, let it have its full fruit or effect. And what is the fruit which the Spirit of God is accustomed to produce hereby in the heart of a believer? One immediate fruit of patience is peace. A sweet tranquillity of mind, a serenity of spirit that can never be found unless where patience reigns. And this peace often rises into joy. Even in the midst of various temptations, those that are enabled "in . . . patience possess ye your souls" (Luke 21:19) can witness not only quietness of spirit but triumph and exultation. This both

> Lays the rough paths of peevish nature even,
> And opens in each breast a little heaven.

How lively is the account that the apostle Peter gives not only of the peace and joy but of the hope and love that God works in those patient sufferers "who are kept by the power of God through faith unto salvation" (1 Peter 1:5). Indeed he appears herein to have an eye to this very passage of St. James: "Though now for a season, . . . ye are in heaviness through manifold temptations [the very word ποικιλοις πειρασμοις]: that the trial of your faith [the same expression that was used by St. James] . . . might be found unto praise and honour and glory at the appearing of Jesus Christ: Whom having not seen, ye love; in whom, though now ye see him not, yet believing, ye rejoice with joy unspeakable and full of glory" (1 Peter 1:6–8). See here the peace, the joy, and the love, which, through the mighty power of God, are the fruit or "work of patience"!

And as peace, hope, joy, and love are the fruits of patience, both springing from and confirmed by it, so is also rational, genuine *courage,* which indeed cannot subsist without patience. The brutal courage, or rather fierceness, of a lion may probably spring from impatience. But true fortitude, the courage of a man, springs from just the contrary temper. Christian *zeal* is likewise confirmed and increased by patience, and so is *activity* in every good work. The same Spirit incites us to be *patient in bearing ill and doing well* makes us equally willing to do and suffer the whole will of God.

But what is the *perfect work* of patience? Is it anything less than the "perfect love of God," constraining us to love every soul of man even "as Christ . . . loved us" (Eph. 5:2)? Is it not the whole of religion, the whole "mind . . . which was also in Christ Jesus" (Phil. 2:5)? Is it not "the renewal of our soul in the image of God, after the likeness of him that created us" (see Col. 3:10)? And is not the fruit of this the constant resignation of ourselves, body and spirit, to God, entirely giving up all we are, all we have, and all we love as a holy sacrifice, acceptable to God through the Son of His love? It seems this is "the perfect work of patience," consequent upon the trial of our faith.

But how does this work differ from that gracious work which is wrought in every believer when he first finds redemption in the blood of Jesus, even the remission of his sins? Many persons that are not only upright of heart, but that fear, no, and love God, have not spoken warily upon this head, not according to the oracles of God. They have spoken of the work of sanctification, taking the word in its full sense as if it were quite of another kind, as if it differed entirely from that which is wrought in justification. But this is a great and dangerous mistake and has a natural tendency to make us undervalue that glorious work of God which was wrought in us when we were justified. Whereas in that moment when we are justified freely by His grace, when we are accepted through the Beloved, we are born again, born from above, born *of* the Spirit. And there is as great a change wrought in our souls when we are born of the Spirit as was wrought in our bodies when we are born of a woman. There is, in that hour, a general change from inward sinfulness to inward holiness. The love of the creature is changed to the love of the Creator; the love of the world into the love of God. Earthly desires–the desire of the flesh, the desire of the eyes, and the pride of life–are, in that instant, changed by the mighty power of God into heavenly desires. The whirlwind of our will is stopped in its mid career and sinks down into the will of God. Pride and haughtiness subside into lowliness of heart, as do anger, with all turbulent and unruly passions, into calmness, meekness, and gentleness. In a word, the earthly, sensual, devilish mind gives place to the "mind . . . which was also in Christ Jesus."

Well, but what more than this can be implied in entire sanctification? It does not imply any new *kind* of holiness. Let no man imagine this. From the moment we are justified until we give up our spirits to God, love is the fulfilling of the Law, of the whole evangelical Law, which took the place of the Adamic law when the first promise of the seed of the woman was made. Love is the sum of Christian sanctification. It is the one *kind* of holiness that is found only in various *degrees* in the believers who are distinguished by St. John into "fathers . . . young men . . . little children" (1 John 2:13). The difference between one and the other properly lies in the degree of love. And herein there is as great a difference in the spiritual as in the natural sense between fathers, young men, and babes.

Everyone that is born of God, though he be as yet only a "babe in Christ," has the love of God in his heart–the love of his neighbor, together with lowliness, meekness, and resignation. But all of these are then in a low degree in proportion to the degree of his faith. The faith of a babe in Christ is weak, generally mingled with doubts or fears–with doubts, whether he has not deceived himself; or fear, that he shall not endure to the end. And if, in order to prevent those perplexing doubts or to remove those tormenting fears, he catches hold of the opinion that a true believer cannot make shipwreck of the faith, experience will sooner or later show that it is merely the staff of a broken reed that will be so far from sustaining him that it will only enter into his hand and pierce it. But to return, in the same proportion as he grows in faith, he grows in holiness. He increases in love, lowliness, meekness in every part of the image of God, until it pleases God, after he is thoroughly convinced of inbred sin, of the total corruption of his nature, to take it all away; to purify his heart and cleanse him from all unrighteousness; to fulfill that promise which He made first to His ancient people, and in them to the Israel of God in all ages: "The LORD thy God will circumcise thine heart, and the heart of thy seed, to love the LORD thy God with all thine heart, and with all thy soul" (Deut. 30:6).

It is not easy to conceive what a difference there is between that which he experiences now and that which he experienced before. Until this universal change was wrought in his soul, all his holiness was *mixed.* He was humble, but not entirely; his humility was mixed with pride. He was meek, but his meekness was frequently interrupted by anger or some uneasy and turbulent passion. His love of God was frequently damped by the love of some creature–the love of his neighbor, by evil surmising, or some thought, if not temper, contrary to love. His will was not wholly melted down into the will of God. But although in general he could say, "I come 'not to do mine own will, but the will of him that sent me'" (John 6:38), yet now and then nature rebelled, and he could not clearly say, "Father, . . . not as I will, but as thou wilt" (Matt. 26:39). His whole soul is now consistent with itself; there is no jarring string. All his passions flow in a continual stream with an even tenor to God. To him that is entered into this rest, you may truly say,

> Calm thou ever art within,
> All unruffled, all serene!

There is no mixture of any contrary affections. All is peace and harmony after. Being filled with love, there is no more interruption of it than of the beating of his heart. Continual love bringing continual joy in the Lord, he rejoices evermore. He converses continually with the God whom he loves, to whom in everything he gives thanks. And as he now loves God with all his heart, soul, mind, and strength, so Jesus now reigns alone in his heart, the Lord of every motion there.

But it may be inquired, in what manner does God work this entire and universal change in the soul of a believer? In what manner does God work this strange work, which so many will not believe, though we declare it unto them? Does He work it gradually by slow degrees or instantaneously in a moment? How many are the disputes upon this head, even among the children of God. And so there will be after all that ever was or ever can be said upon it. For many will still say with the famous Jew, *Non persuadebis, etiamsi persuaseris.* That is, "Thou shalt not persuade me, though thou dost persuade me." And they will be the more resolute herein because the Scriptures are silent upon the subject, because the point is not determined, at least not in express terms, in any part of the oracles of God. Every man, therefore, may abound in his own sense provided he will allow the same liberty to his neighbor, provided he will not be angry at those who differ from his opinion nor entertain hard thoughts concerning them. Permit me likewise to add one thing more. Be the change instantaneous or gradual, see that you never rest until it is wrought in your own soul if you desire to dwell with God in glory.

This premised, in order to throw what light I can upon this interesting question, I will simply relate what I have seen myself in the course of many years. Forty-four or forty-five years ago when I had no distinct views of what the apostle meant by exhorting us to "leave the principles of the doctrine of Christ, let us go unto perfection" (Heb. 6:1), two or three persons in London, whom I knew to be truly sincere, desired to give me an account of their experience. It appeared exceeding strange, being different from any that I had heard before, but exactly similar to the preceding account of entire sanctification. The next year, two or three more persons at Bristol and two or three in Kingswood, coming to me severally, gave me exactly the same account of their experience. A few years after, I desired all those in London who made the same profession to come to me all together at the Foundry that I might be thoroughly satisfied. I desired that man of God, Thomas Walsh, to give us the meeting there. When we met, first one of us and then the other asked them the most searching questions we could devise. They answered everyone without hesitation and with the utmost simplicity so that we were fully persuaded. They did not deceive themselves. In the years 1759, 1760, 1761, and 1762, their numbers multiplied exceedingly not only in London and Bristol but in various parts of Ireland as well as England. Not trusting to the testimony of others, I carefully examined most of these myself. In London alone I found six hundred fifty-two members of our society who were exceedingly clear in their experience and of whose testimony I could see no reason to doubt. I believe no year has passed since that time wherein God has not wrought the same work in many others. Sometimes in one part of England or Ireland, sometimes in another—as "the wind bloweth where it listeth" (John 3:8)—everyone of these (after the most careful inquiry, I have not found one exception either in Great Britain or Ireland) has declared that their deliverance from sin was *instantaneous,* that the change was wrought in a moment. Had half of these, or one third, or one in twenty, declared it was *gradually* wrought in *them,* I should have believed this with regard to *them* and thought that *some* were gradually sanctified and some instantaneously. But as I have not found, in so long a space of time, a single person speaking thus, as all who believe they are sanctified declare with one voice that the change was wrought in a moment, I cannot but believe that sanctification is commonly, if not always, an *instantaneous* work.

But however that question be decided, whether sanctification in the full sense of the word be wrought instantaneously or gradually, how may we attain to it? "What shall *we* do," said the Jews to our Lord, "that we might work the works of God?" (John 6:28). His answer will suit those that ask, What shall we do that this work of God may be wrought in us? "This is the work of God, that ye believe on him whom he hath sent" (v. 29). On this one work all the others depend. Believe on the Lord Jesus Christ, and all His wisdom, power, and faithfulness are engaged on your side. In this, as in all other instances, "by grace are ye saved through faith" (Eph. 2:8). Sanctification also is "not of works, lest any man should boast" (v. 9). "It is the gift of God" (v. 8) and is to be received by plain, simple faith. Suppose you are now laboring to "abstain from all appearance of evil" (1 Thess. 5:22), "zealous of good works" (Titus 2:14), and walking diligently and carefully in all the ordinances of God, there is then only one point remaining: the voice of God to your soul is, "Believe and be saved" (Luke 8:12). First, believe that God has *promised* to save you from all sin and to fill you with all holiness. Secondly, believe that "he is *able* also to save them to the uttermost that come unto God by him" (Heb. 7:25). Thirdly, believe that He is *willing,* as well as able, to save you to the uttermost, to purify you from all sin, and fill up all your heart with love. Believe, fourthly, that He is not only able, but willing to do it now! Not when you come to die, not at any distant time, not tomorrow, but *today.* He will then enable you to believe *it is done* according to His Word. And then "patience [shall] have her perfect work, that ye may be perfect and entire, wanting nothing."

Ye shall then be perfect. The apostle seems to mean by this expression, τελειοι, you shall be wholly delivered from every evil work, word, thought, desire, passion, temper, inbred corruption, and from all remains of the carnal mind and the body of sin. You shall be renewed in the spirit of your mind, in every right temper, after the image of Him that created you in righteousness and true holiness. You shall be *entire,* ολοκληροι (the same word that the apostle uses to the Christians in Thessalonica). This seems to refer not so much to the kind as to the degree of holiness, as if he had said, "Ye shall enjoy as high a degree of holiness as is consistent with your present state of pilgrimage." You shall *want nothing.* The Lord being your Shepherd, your Father, your Redeemer, your Sanctifier, your God, and your all will feed you with the bread of heaven and give you meat enough. He will lead you forth beside the waters of comfort and keep you every moment, so that loving Him with all your heart (which is the sum of all perfection), you will "rejoice evermore. Pray without ceasing. In everything give thanks" (1 Thess. 5:16–18), until "an entrance shall be ministered unto you abundantly into the everlasting kingdom of our Lord and Saviour Jesus Christ" (2 Peter 1:11)!

NOTES

The Gentleness of God

George H. Morrison (1866–1928) assisted the great Alexander Whyte in Edinburgh, pastored two churches, and then, in 1902, became pastor of the distinguished Wellington Church on University Avenue in Glasgow, Scotland. His preaching drew great crowds; in fact, people had to line up an hour before the services to ensure that they got seats in the large auditorium. Morrison was a master of imagination in preaching, yet his messages are solidly biblical.

From his many published volumes of sermons, I have chosen this message, found in *The Weaving of Glory,* published by Hodder and Stoughton, London.

10

The Gentleness of God

Thy gentleness hath made me great. (Psalm 18:35)

WHAT EXACTLY MAY BE MEANT BY GREATNESS is a question that we need not linger to discuss. It is enough that the writer of this verse was conscious that he had been lifted to that eminence. That he had been in very sore distress is clear from the earlier verses of this chapter. His heart had fainted; his efforts had been vain; his hopes had flickered and sunk into their ashes. And then mysteriously, but very certainly, he had been carried upward to light and power and liberty, and now he is looking back over it all. That it was God who had so raised him up was, of course, as clear to him as noonday. He had sent up his cry to heaven in the dark, and to that cry his greatness was the answer. But what impressed him as he surveyed it all was not the infinite power of the Almighty. It was rather the amazing and unceasing gentleness wherewith that infinite power had been displayed. "Thy gentleness hath made me great," he cried. That was the outstanding and arresting feature. Tracing the way by which he had been led, he saw conspicuous a gentle ministry. And so tonight, in interpreting in the light of Christ that old expression, I should like to speak on the gentleness of God.

Let me say in passing that that wonderful conception is really peculiar to the Bible. I know no deity in any sacred book that exhibits such an attribute as that. Of course, when you have many gods, it is always possible that one of them be gentle. When the whole world is tenanted with spirits, some of them doubtless will be gentle spirits. But that is a very different thing indeed from saying that the one Lord of heaven and earth has that in His heart which we can dimly picture under the human attribute of gentleness. No prophets save the prophets of Israel ever conceived the gentleness of God. To no other poets save these Jewish poets was the thought of heavenly gentleness revealed. And so when we delight in this great theme, we are dwelling on something eminently biblical, something that makes us, with all our Christian liberty, a debtor to this hour to the Jew.

Now if we wish to grasp the wonder of God's gentleness, there are one or two things we ought to do. We ought, for instance, ever to lay it against the background of the divine omnipotence. You know quite well that the greater the power, the more arresting does gentleness become. As might advances and energy increases, so always the more notable is gentleness. It is far more striking in a mailed warrior than in a mother with her woman's heart. It is far more impressive in the lord of armies than in some retired and ineffectual dreamer. The mightier the power a man commands, the more compelling is his trait of gentleness. If he be a tyrant of a million subjects, a touch of tenderness is thrilling. And it is when we think of the infinite might of God, who is King of Kings and Lord of Lords, that we realize the wonder of our text. It is He who calls out the stars by number and makes the pillars of the heaven to shake. And when He works, no man can stay His hand nor say to Him, What do you do? And it is this Ruler, infinite in power, before whom the princes of the earth are vanity, who is exquisitely and forever gentle.

Again, to feel the wonder of it, we must set it against the background of God's righteousness. It is when we hear the seraphs crying holy, that we thrill to the thought of the gentleness of God. There is a kind of gentleness–we are all familiar with it–that springs from an easy and uncaring tolerance. It is the happy good-nature of those characters to whom both right and wrong are nebulous. Never inspired by any love of goodness and never touched by any hate of evil, it is not difficult to walk the world with a certain smiling tolerance of everybody. Now there have been nations whose gods were of that kind. Their gentleness was the index of their weakness. Living immoral lives in their Olympus, why should they worry about man's immorality? But I need hardly linger to point out to you that the one radical thing about the Jewish God–the one unchanging feature of His being–was that He was infinitely and forever holy. He was of purer eyes than to behold iniquity. "The soul that sinneth," said the prophet, "it shall die" (Ezek. 18:4, 20). And He visits the sins of the fathers on the children, even unto the third and fourth generation. All this was graven on the Jewish heart and inwrought into the Jewish history. Yet could the psalmist sing in his great hour, "Thy gentleness hath made me great." I beg of you, therefore, never to imagine that the gentleness of God is but an easy tolerance. Whatever it be, it certainly is not *that,* as life sooner or later shows to every man. Whatever it be, it leans against the background of a righteousness that burns as does a fire, and I say that helps us to feel the wonder of it.

Well now, if the gentleness of God be a great fact, we shall expect to light on traces of it everywhere. And I think that the more we dwell upon His handiwork, the more clear to us does it become.

Think, for example, of the realm of nature–of this spacious world in which we dwell. It is not only eloquent of power, it is eloquent also of the hiding of that power. Creation in a day may tell of power, but I want to know more of the Creator than just power. I want to trace in the broad world around me foregleams of that God I find in Christ. And it is when I learn how the Creator moves in infinite delicacy through countless ages that I find in nature something more than power—I find there the gentleness of God. There is not a daisy in any summer meadow but could say, "Thy gentleness hath made me great." There is not a bird that flies across the heaven but could take up and carry on the cry. For bird and flower and sun and moon and star are what they are, *not* because God is mighty only, but because the hand of God through ages has been unceasingly and exquisitely gentle.

The same jewel upon the bosom of omnipotence flashes out as we survey the Bible. The Bible is really one long record of the amazing gentleness of God. Other features of the divine character may be more immediately impressive there. And reading hastily, one might easily miss the revelation of a gentle God. Yet so might one walking beside the sea, where hammers were ringing in the village workshop, easily miss the underlying music of the waves ceaselessly breaking on the shore. But the waves are breaking although the hammers drown them, and the gentleness of God is always there. It is there—not very far away—at the heart of all the holiness and sovereignty. It is there where the fire of His anger waxes hot and His judgments are abroad upon the earth, and men are crying, "It is a fearful thing to fall into the hands of the living God" (Heb. 10:31).

Take, for instance, that opening Scripture of Adam and of his sin and exile. Whatever else it means, it means unquestionably that God is angry with disobedient man. And, yet, at the back of it what an unequalled tenderness, as of a father pitying his children and loving them with a love that never burns so bright as in the bitter hour of necessary punishment. Losing his innocence, in the love of God Adam found his calling and his crown. He fell to rise into a world of toil and through his toil to realize his powers. So looking backward, through that bitter discipline, unparadised but not unshepherded, he too could surely say with David, "Thy gentleness hath made me great."

Or think again of the story of the Exodus, that true foundation of the Jewish race. It took one night to take Israel out of

Egypt, but forty years to take Egypt out of Israel. And while that night when the first-born were slain was dark and terrible with the mighty power of God, what are those forty years of desert wandering but the witness of the gentleness of heaven? Leaving Egypt a company of slaves, they had to win the spirit of the free. Leaving it shiftless, they had to win reliance. Leaving it cowardly, they had to learn to conquer. Leaving it mean, they were to reach to greatness by and by. And looking back on it all, what could they say but this, "Thy gentleness hath made me great." Never forget that in its age-long story the Bible reveals the gentleness of God. Hinted at in every flower that blossoms, it is evidently declared in Holy Scripture. It is seen in Adam and in Abraham. It is seen in the wilderness journey of the Israelites. It is found in the choicest oracles of prophecy and in the sweetest music of the psalms.

I think, too, that as life advances, we can all set to our seal that that is true. We all discover, as the psalmist did, how mighty has been the gentleness of heaven. In the ordinary senses of the word, you and I may not be reckoned great. We have neither been born great, nor have we come to greatness, nor has greatness been thrust upon us. And yet it may be that for you and me life is a nobler thing than it was long ago, and truth is more queenly and duty more august than in a bypassed day we can remember. We may not have won any striking moral victories, yet has our life leaned to the victorious side. We have not conquered yet all that we hoped to conquer, yet our will is serving us better through the years. There are still impurities that lift up their heads and still passions that have to be brought to heel, yet it may be that you and I tonight are nearer the sunrise than ten years ago. If, then, that be so with you, I bid you halt a moment this Sabbath evening. I bid you look back on the way that you have come and think of all that life has meant for you. For if you do it, and do it in sincerity, I believe that you, like the old psalmist, will go out into the lighted streets and whisper, "Thy gentleness hath made me great."

Think of the temptations that would have overcome you had

not God in His gentleness taken them away. Think of the courage you got when things were dark and of the doors that opened when every way seemed barred. Think of the unworthy things that you have done which God in His infinite gentleness has hidden—of the love that inspired you and of the hope that came to you when not far distant was the sound of breakers. You, too, if you are a man at all, can lift up your eyes and cry out, *God is just.* It may be you can do more than that, and lifting up your voice say, *God is terrible.* But if you have eyes to see, and a heart to understand, there is something more that you can say, for you can whisper, "To me, in pardoning, shielding mercy, God has been infinitely and divinely gentle." If every lily of the field lifting its head can say, "Thy gentleness hath made me great," if every sparrow chirping on the eaves is only echoing that meadow music, then I do feel that you and I, who are of more value to God than many sparrows, owe more than we shall ever understand to the abounding gentleness of heaven.

Now it seems to me that this gentleness of God reveals certain precious things about Him. It reveals, for instance, and it is rooted in, His perfect understanding of His children. There is a saying with which you are familiar. It is that to know all is to forgive all. That is an apothegm, and like all apothegms, it is not commensurate with the whole truth. Yet as a simple matter of experience, so much of our harshness has its rise in ignorance that such a saying is sure of immortality—to know all is to forgive all. How often you and I, after some judgment, have said to ourselves, *If I had only known.* Something is told us that we knew nothing of, and instantly there is a revulsion in our hearts. And we retract the judgment that we passed, and we bitterly regret we were unfeeling and say we never would have spoken so had we but known. The more we know—I speak in a broad way—the more we know, the more gentle we become. The more we understand what human life is, the more does a great pitifulness reach us. And I take it that it is just because our heavenly Father sees right down into the secret heart that He is so greatly and pitifully gentle. For He knows our frame and remembers we are dust, and He puts all our tears into His bottle. And there is not a cross we carry and not a thought we think but He is acquainted with it altogether. And all we have inherited by birth, of power or weakness, of longing or of fear—I take it that all *that* is known to the God of Abraham, Isaac, and Jacob.

And, then again, it reveals this to us—it reveals our abiding value in His sight. It tells us, as almost nothing else can tell us, that we, His children, are precious in His eyes. There are certain books upon my shelves at home with which I scarcely trouble to be gentle. I am not vexed when I see them tossed about nor when they are handled in an untender way. But there are other books that I could never handle without a certain reverence and care, and I am gentle because they are of value to me. And the singular thing is that these precious volumes are not always the volumes that are most finely bound. Some of them are little tattered creatures that a respectable servant longs to light the fire with. But every respectable servant of a book lover comes to learn this at least about her master, that his ways, like those of another Master, are mysterious and past finding out. For that little volume, tattered though it be, may have memories that make it infinitely precious—memories of schooldays or of college days, memories of the hillside where first we read it. It may be the first Shakespeare that we ever had or the first Milton that we ever handled, and we shall handle it gently to the end because to us it is a precious thing. So I take it God is gentle because you and I are precious in His sight. He is infinitely patient with the worst of us because He values the worst of us so dearly. And if you want to know how great that value is, then go home and read this text again: "For God so loved the world, that he gave his only begotten Son, that whosoever believeth in him should not perish, but have everlasting life" (John 3:16).

Practical Christianity

Charles Simeon (1759–1836) was ordained in the Church of England in 1783 and ministered at the Church of the Holy Trinity, Cambridge, until his death. Under his leadership, the church became a vibrant center for evangelical preaching, evangelism, and world missions. He was one of the founders of the Church Missionary Society and greatly influenced Henry Martyn, missionary to India and Persia (Iran). Simeon said that he had three purposes in his ministry: to exalt Jesus Christ, to humble sinners, and to promote holy living.

This message was taken from *Evangelical Preaching,* a collection of Simeon's addresses edited by James Houston and published in 1986 by Multnomah Press.

11

Practical Christianity

The fruit of the Spirit is in all goodness and righteousness and truth. (Ephesians 5:9)

MANY PEOPLE ARE PREJUDICED against the writings of the apostle Paul, as though they contain nothing but dissertations about predestination and election. It is as if all they were calculated to do was to drive people into a depression rather than to improve their morals. But there are no writings in the whole of Scripture that are more practical than his. It is true that he unfolds the whole mystery of godliness more fully and deeply than the others. He seems to have been raised up of God for that very end, that the theory of religion might be more distinctly known. But in all his epistles he has special regard to the interests of morality. He sets a standard never known before, and for the practice of which he adduces motives that have never been so appreciated. In not one of his epistles does he maintain more strongly those doctrines which are thought to be so objectionable than in this. Yet half of the epistle is preoccupied with exhortations to holiness in all its different bearings and relations.

In the words we have before us, we have what I may call a *compendium* or *summary* of Christian morals. And that we may know what practical Christianity really is, I will describe it as follows:

Note Its Distinctive Purposes

Sanctification in both heart and life is the great end of the gospel. It is a vital part of what is revealed to us in redemption. Here he sets forth some of the things that it includes:

Goodness. This is the one all-comprehensive character of the Godhead. It shines forth in all his works. It meets us wherever we turn our eyes. "The earth is full of the goodness of the LORD" (Ps. 33:5). The effect of the gospel is to transform us into His image. It does this by creating the gospel in our hearts and calling it forth in our lives. Under the influence of this divine principle, we shall seek to promote the happiness of all around us. Whatever is kind and lovely and of good report, in such a spirit and temper of the mind we shall cultivate it utterly and exercise it always. There will be no trouble that we will not labor to alleviate. There is no need that we shall not endeavor to supply. To be "good, and doest good" (119:68), even like God Himself, will be the height of our ambition and the very end of our lives.

Righteousness. While goodness is spontaneous, acting irrespective of any particular claim which people may have upon us, "righteousness" has respect to the obligations that we have in order to "render . . . to all their dues" (Rom. 13:7). This is also the way in which the gospel forms within us. It stirs us up, both in word and deed, to act toward others as we in a change of circumstances should think it right for them to do to us. There is in the heart of man a selfishness that disposes him to see everything with partial eyes. It magnifies his own rights and overlooks the rights of others. This disposition the gospel will subdue and mortify. And in its place it will establish a principle of universal equity that will weigh the claims of others with exactness and prompt us always rather to "suffer wrong than to do wrong."

Truth. This is the perfection of Christian morals, or rather the bond that keeps all the other graces in their place (Eph. 6:14). Where the gospel has done its perfect work, there will be a spirit "in whom is no guile" (John 1:47). The Christian has a transparent character. He appears as he is, and is as he appears.

You will note that in the immediate context of our text the apostle says, "Walk as children of light: (for the fruit of the Spirit is in all goodness and righteousness and truth)" (Eph. 5:8–9). Now, these three graces mentioned in the text are represented as constituting light, or at least as comprehending all that is contained in that image. Now, of all things in the whole creation, light is the most pure (for it is incapable of defilement). It is the most innocent (for it injures nothing which has not, through its own weakness, an aversion to its rays). It is also the most beneficial (for there is nothing in the universe, whether animal or vegetable, that is not nourished and refreshed by it). Reverse the order of these statements and you see how light beams forth in our text. It embodies all the purity of truth, all the innocence of righteousness, and all the beneficence of active goodness.

But in order to understand Christianity properly we must,

Trace It to Its Source

It does not come from nature. For the natural man cannot attain to it. It is "the fruit of the Spirit," even of that very Spirit who raised up our Lord Jesus Christ himself from the dead (Eph. 1:19–20).

It is the Spirit who alone infuses life into us. We are by nature "dead in trespasses and sins" (Eph. 2:1). But it is the Spirit who quickens us that we may live to our God. It is true, indeed, that having been "baptized into Christ" (Gal. 3:27), we have become by profession branches of the living vine. But then we are only as dead and withered branches that can produce no fruit. We will shortly be broken off and cast into the fire (John 15:2, 6). It is the Spirit alone who engrafts us into Christ as living branches. He causes us to receive from Christ that divine energy, so that we are able to bring forth fruit to His glory. Christ came that we "might have life, and . . . might have it more abundantly" (John 10:10). It is by the operation of His Spirit that we receive it. It is by the mighty working of that Spirit in our souls that we display its energies (Col. 1:29).

It is the Spirit who suggests to our mind those motives that alone can stimulate us to exertion. He reveals the Lord Jesus Christ in our hearts (Gal. 1:15–16). He glorifies Christ within us, taking of the things that are His and showing them to us (John 16:14). He sheds abroad in our hearts the love of Christ (Rom. 5:5), which alone can constrain us to devote ourselves unreservedly to Him (2 Cor. 5:14). Until we receive this impulse, we are satisfied with formal services and a partial obedience. But when we are thus enabled to comprehend something of the unbounded love of Christ, we can rest in nothing, until we are filled with all the fullness of God (Eph. 3:18–19).

It is the Spirit who assists us in all our endeavors. Whatever we may have attained, we still have no sufficiency in ourselves. Indeed, we shall put our hands to the work, but we can accomplish nothing until the Holy Spirit strengthens us with might in our inward man (Col. 1:11). Taking, as it were, one end of our burden to bear it with us, He "helpeth our infirmities" and gives us His own effectual aid (Rom. 8:26). That is why these graces are properly called "the fruit of the Spirit." For they could not be produced without Him and are invariably the result of His agency in our souls. It is He who, as our church well expresses it, "works in us, that we may have a good will; and works with us when we have that good will" (Tenth Article).

It must be confessed, however, that there is a resemblance of this holiness found in those who have not the Holy Spirit. So it is necessary to,

Distinguish It from All Counterfeits

It must be admitted that in many remarkable people there are found virtues they have naturally that resemble the graces described above. In some there is the quality of kindness or a sense of fairness or a high degree of integrity. Reasonably we can ask, "What distinguishes these traits from the 'fruit of the Spirit'?" The answer is that we can only look on the outward act, and externally they may be very difficult to distinguish. But to God, who sees the heart, they are as different from each other as light from darkness. For of these counterfeits I must say the following:

They proceed from man, and man alone. Man needs no particular communication of the Spirit to enable him to perform them. The light of reason points them out as commendable virtues, while the strength of a person's resolution is enough for performing accordingly. Such people never need to pray to God for His Spirit nor do they feel need of divine help. But the graces referred to in our text are "the fruit of the Spirit." They never were nor ever can be produced in any other way than by His Almighty agency.

They have respect to man, and to man alone. The worldling, however virtuous, acts not to God nor has any distinct desire to fulfill the will of God. He reckons that as a member of society he has duties to perform. Therefore he performs them solely from a human perspective and context. He has no other perspective than that of an intelligent heathen. But the Christian aims at "*all* goodness, righteousness, and truth." He views them as the Lord Jesus Christ did and makes the outward discharge of them as the Lord Jesus Christ did, subservient to higher and nobler ends than man himself. As a servant of the Lord Jesus Christ he has to advance Christ's interests in the salvation of men. So it is a less significant matter to exercise kindness to men as such, if he may not, according to his ability, also promote their spiritual and eternal welfare.

They are done for man, and man alone. A worldling is only concerned to please his fellowman and for man alone. He wants to establish a good character before them. If he can do so, he is satisfied. Standing high in his own esteem, and in the esteem of others, is all he wants. But the Christian desires that God, and God alone, may be glorified. He does not seek the applause of men but of God. He cherishes no conceit about himself and his imagined superiority. Much less does he go about trying to establish his own self-righteousness by which to stand before God. Instead of self-admiration, he acknowledges that his attainments come from God and gives glory to God. Indeed, the more he is able to do so, the more indebted he becomes to God. So he dare not to sacrifice to his own net, or burn incense to his own drag (Hab. 1:16). Rather he accounts himself, after all, as an unprofitable servant, saying, "not unto us, O LORD, not unto us, but unto thy name give glory" (Ps. 115:1).

Now whether we can discern the difference between these two attitudes in others or not, we can certainly distinguish them in ourselves. So we can easily discern "whose we are, and whom we serve." I cannot urge ourselves strongly enough to be jealous over ourselves so that we do not make the terrible mistake of confusing the virtues of the flesh for the graces of the Spirit, in case having a name to live we prove to be really dead (Rev. 3:1).

The Cultivation

For the cultivation of this subject, notice the three following points:

How excellent is our religion! Those who merely view Christianity as a system of doctrines, irrespective of what effects they should have upon us, have a very erroneous perspective. So I will readily grant that mysteries, however grand they may be, are of little value if they bring no sanctifying effect within us. But look at the change the Spirit can make in the life of the believer. See how such poor, selfish creatures can be transformed into the likeness of Jesus Christ, walking in the world as He walked. Go and look in the world, into the family situation and into the privacy of his life, to see the dispositions and habits of the true Christian. How can one see this, if only with a glance, and not admire such a religion from which it flows? I charge you, therefore, not to be content with a partial view of

Christianity, merely looking for doctrinal orthodoxy that may be also doctrinally speculative. No, rather see it in all its practical efficiency, and you will be ready to respect it with honor and love.

How easily we may find out our true state before God! We shall surely find out without much difficulty what our attitude and tempers really are. We shall know whether or not we are in the daily habit of imploring God to help us grow spiritually. Yet our natural temperaments differ so greatly that we cannot be absolutely certain whether someone is a natural or a spiritual person. This can only be learned from the struggles he has and the victories he achieves under the influence of the Holy Spirit. At all events, we may be sure that where there is no delight in doing good to the souls of men, where in our conduct toward others there is willful inconsistency or lack of simplicity and godly sincerity in our motives and principles, then we are not Christians. I pray you will use this test on yourselves (2 Cor. 13:5). Do so, that in the end your hopes will not be disappointed (Ps. 139:23–24).

How wonderful is our allotted path! I do not say that you will not have times of humiliation, for they come to the best of us. But for the daily course of your lives, you need only follow our text. See the daily Christian in his daily walk. "Goodness and righteousness and truth" are embodied in him. Like the sun's rays, he diffuses light and happiness all around him. This is what it means to "walk in the light, as [God] is in the light" (1 John 1:7). This is to honor God. This is to adorn the gospel. This is to fulfill what Christ came Himself to do in the world. This is to possess a meetness for the heavenly inheritance. So let those who do not possess true religion condemn it if they will. But I am certain that when viewed aright, "her ways are ways of pleasantness, and all her paths are peace" (Prov. 3:17).

Faithful Stewardship

Charles Haddon Spurgeon (1834–1892) is undoubtedly the most famous minister of the nineteenth century. Converted in 1850, he united with the Baptists and soon began to preach in various places. He became pastor of the Baptist church in Waterbeach, England, in 1851, and three years later he was called to the decaying Park Street Church, London. Within a short time, the work began to prosper, a new church was built and dedicated in 1861, and Spurgeon became London's most popular preacher. In 1855, he began to publish his sermons weekly; today they make up the fifty-seven volumes of *The Metropolitan Tabernacle Pulpit*. He founded a pastor's college and several orphanages.

This sermon was taken from *The Metropolitan Tabernacle Pulpit,* volume 41.

CHARLES HADDON SPURGEON

12

Faithful Stewardship

Moreover it is required in stewards, that a man be found faithful.
(1 Corinthians 4:2)

IT IS WELL THAT OUR DEAR FRIENDS should make a right account of us. Paul says in the verse preceding our text, "Let a man so account of us" (1 Cor. 4:1), for there are some who make a wrong reckoning as to the ministers of the gospel. Some go to an extreme, for they glory in men. One glories in Paul, who is so deep in doctrine; another in Cephas, who is so energetic and plain-spoken; another in Apollos, who is so exceedingly eloquent and mighty in the Scriptures. But Paul says in the latter verses of the third chapter, "Let no man glory in men. For all things are yours; Whether Paul, or Apollos, or Cephas, or the world, or life, or death, or things present, or things to come; all are yours; And ye are Christ's; and Christ is God's" (3:21). You do not belong to your ministers; you must not put yourselves down as followers of them. You belong to Christ, and Christ Himself and all His ministers belong to you.

But while some erred in thinking too much of their ministers, as no doubt they still do—God deliver them from such a delusion—there were, no doubt, others who erred in not thinking enough of them, not appreciating their position and condition so as to sympathize with them and pray for them. Had they known to what a responsible office they were called and what was required at their hands, they would lovingly have borne them upon their hearts and gone with their names to the mercy seat in continual prayer. Hence, it is very important that men should so account of us as to judge of us correctly; so that, while they do not rely upon us in any wrong sense, they may at the same time feel an affectionate sympathy with us and constantly bear us up before the throne of grace.

Paul goes on to tell us how we ought to account of the ministers of Christ. The word should be "servants" of Christ. There is a great respectability about the word "minister" that really does not belong to it. If you take it to pieces, it means an under-rower, one of those Inca who had to take an oar on the lowest benches of the trireme. There were three benches for the rowers, and it was a hard task for all who were at the oars. But to the under-rowers, who had to bend to their work in the most trying position as they sent the galley flying through the water, it was stern toil indeed. Now, God's ministers, if they act as they should do, are under-rowers of Christ. They are tugging away at a very heavy oar, and they may well ask you to pray that, as they use up their strength, fresh force may be imparted to them from the God of all power that they may not labor in vain nor spend their strength for nothing.

We ask men, therefore, to account of us as servants, not as masters. The word "bishop" has come to have a wonderful signification about it which is not in the least degree scriptural. We are simply to be shepherds of the sheep, and a shepherd is no great lord. He is the servant of all the sheep. Though he leads them, it is by going first, taking the brunt of all that comes, and finding out the best places for them to feed and to rest. Let a man so account of us as servants. But not merely as servants to the church, certainly not as servants to men, but as servants of Christ. That is our honor as ministers, we serve the Lord Jesus Christ, the best of masters. But, as He deserves to have the best of servants, the responsibility of the position weighs down the honor attached to it. Oh, if they who serve men should serve them faithfully, how much more should they be found faithful who are the servants of Christ!

Then the apostle adds that men are to account of us as stewards, and it is about that office that I am going to speak to you: "It is required in stewards, that a man be found faithful." Although my text no doubt refers, in the first place, to those who labor in word and doctrine, to whom it is a life's vocation, yet all the people of God are stewards. Each child of God, in his own way and in his own place, should reckon that whatever gift he has should be used for the Lord Jesus Christ and laid out for Him. He should also recollect that he is made one of the Lord's stewards and that it is required of him that he be found faithful. And I may even add that every unconverted man has a stewardship to fulfill. As God's creature, he is bound to be God's servant. At the last great day he will have to give an account of every opportunity and capacity for service which God has given to him, and woe to him if he be found an unfaithful steward in the day of his Lord's reckoning!

If I should seem to speak rather more about ministers than about anybody else, I will ask you kindly to pick out all that belongs to yourselves, you who are private Christians, and you who are not Christians at all. I pray the Lord to make use of what I say to myself, then to you who are His people, and then to those also who are not His people that they may be pricked to the heart and made to feel how ungenerously they have acted toward the great Lord of the house. To begin, then, I will first ask, *How are we stewards?* Secondly, if stewards, *How are we to behave?* Next, *How are we in danger of misbehaving?* And, lastly, *What will be the result* of right behavior or of misbehavior in those who are stewards?

How Are We Stewards?

Well, Gods ministers are stewards, first, *as appointed to look after other servants.* You know, dear friend, if you are a servant, you have enough to do to mind your own work. But if you happen to be an upper servant, such as a steward is, you have not only your own work to mind, but it is a part of your own work to look after the work of other people. There are some who are so foolish that they look only at the honor of this position. Whereas, if they were wise, they would look more at the responsibility of it. If I had my choice, I would rather look after a horse than look after a man. The second is much the more difficult animal to manage, and to look after many men–oh, this is indeed a difficult task! I had an old friend who was for forty years a shepherd, and after that he became a minister. He lived to be forty years a shepherd in a spiritual sense. I asked him once, "Which was the easier flock to manage? "Oh!" he replied, "the second flock of sheep was a deal more sheepish than the first." I understood what he meant. They say that sheep have as many diseases as there are days in the year, but men have as many complaints as there are minutes in the year. It is not long that they are free from one malady or another. I mean, men and women, all those that belong to the spiritual flock of which the minister is the shepherd, there is a certain form of trouble arising out of each one. True, there is a certain amount of comfort and joy arising out of every Christian, yet there is a measure of difficulty that must come to the steward from every one of his fellow servants. It is by no means a position which any man who understands it might desire for himself. The real steward is one who has been appointed to the position, and if he is not appointed, why he has no right to be a steward at all! It is the great Master of the house who calls this one or that to look after the other servants, and it is from this calling that he has the right to interfere in any respect with them.

Next, notice that the servants of God–whether called ministers or not–those who are really so, are stewards *because they are under the Master's near command.* An ordinary servant in God's house may take his orders from the steward, but the steward takes no order from anybody but the Master. Hence, he is in an evil case, and the household is in an evil case, too, if he does not often resort to the Master, if he does not distinctly recognize his position as an underling of his Master, and if he does not so keep up his daily fellowship with the Master that he himself knows the Master's mind and is able to communicate it to his fellow servants. There are many of you, dear friends, who have around you your children, your servants, your fellow workers. Well, in that respect, you are a steward to them. They have to do a good deal that you tell them. Then do, I pray you—and I speak this to myself as well as to you—do let us wait upon the Master. Let us come forth to speak to our fellow servants, not our own words, but the words of Him who is Master and Lord to the whole household.

How beautifully Jesus, the greatest of all stewards, did this! How constantly He said, "The words that I speak unto you I speak not of myself: but the Father that dwelleth in me, he doeth the works" (John 14:10). He was always referring those who were His brethren back to the great Head of the family, and He did not speak without His Father's authority. Having taken up the position of a subordinate in order to work out our redemption, He continually declared that He was His Father's servant. It is an ill day for us when we begin to think that our thoughts are to be given out in the house instead of the Master's thoughts. It is not for us to deliver our own speculations, but to go straight away to the Word, and by the teaching of the indwelling Spirit to come forth to the people with what we have received not what we have invented. You shall find no power, my brothers and sisters, in doing Christian work unless you keep on doing it as receiving your mission and commission from the great Lord of all. I recollect how McCheyne says, "It is God's Word that saves, not our comment on God's Word." And I am sure that it is so. It is God at the back of the steward who blesses all in the household. But when the steward does not go to the Master and get his orders from Him, he soon puts everything into confusion. He loses his own standing, and he is apt to do desperate mischief to all who are around him.

Then, the true steward *is called upon to give an account,* and if he does it often, so much the better. I am persuaded that, in the things of God as well as between man and man, "short reckonings make long friends." If we will often go to our Master with our service, present it to Him, overhaul it under His divine guidance, confess our shortcomings, and bless Him for every particle of success that has attended it, we shall do much better than if we go on for a long stretch without a reference to Him. Brothers and sisters, you who are teaching your classes of boys or girls, bring your Sunday work to the Lord at the end of the Sabbath. When we have finished a sermon, those of us who stand up to preach, let us not be satisfied until we have brought that piece of our work under our Master's eye. I am sure that if the steward can get to the side of his Master every evening or every morning and say to Him, "We did so-and-so yesterday, and there is so-and-so which we propose to do today," that is the way for the house to be well-ordered. Things go right when there is no absentee landlord and when the great Master is always close at hand and the steward constantly goes to Him with an account of all his work. Let us constantly act thus! We do not live near enough to God, do we? I know that some of you do wait upon Him day and night, and you abide under the shadow of the Almighty. But I fear that there are some workers who forget to do this. We should work with the hands of Martha, but yet keep near the Master with the heart of Mary. We want a combination of activity and meditation. When we get that, when we inwardly retire for consultation with our Lord and then come out actively to labor for our Lord, then shall we be good stewards in the little part of the great house with which he has entrusted us.

Further, a steward is a man who *is put in trust with his master's goods.* This is the main point of his stewardship—nothing is his own, it is all his master's. When he begins to open an account of his own, it is wonderful how apt he is to mistake what is his master's and to call it his own. By-and-by he gets into a muddle and cannot distinguish his master's accounts from his own. Oh, it is a glorious thing when you have no "own," when you do not live for yourself at all but wholly for Christ! Then you will not make any blunders. There will not be any of Christ's property getting into your cash account, so that you will have difficulty in disentangling it. "No man that warreth entangleth himself with the affairs of this life," for he can say, "'Tis done, the great transaction's done, I am my Lord's, and all the business I have here below is His. I have no sub-ends or secondary objects, but all I have and am is for Him." Then it is easy to keep our accounts and to make no mistakes in them.

The true steward is put in trust with his master's property, first, to protect it. Oh, with what earnestness ought we to guard the gospel of Christ! With what holy valor ought we to contend earnestly for the faith once for all delivered to the saints! "Hold fast the form of sound words," wrote Paul to Timothy (2 Tim. 1:13). Not only the words, but the particular form of them that the apostle had delivered; not merely sound doctrine, but the very words in which those doctrines had been made to take shape. The true steward is to defend his master's treasure with his very life. The Lord has put us in trust with the gospel, and all the people of God, in their measure, have also become trustees of those inestimably precious doctrines wherein will be found the glory of God and the salvation of the sons of men. So we are to defend our Master's property.

And next, we are to dispense it. It is the steward who provides for the table of the household; he brings out of that treasury things new and old. He never forgets when the table is spread to put the bread and the salt on it. The bread is Christ Himself, on which we feed, and the salt is the grace of which we cannot have too much. The true steward does not starve the children, but he sees that each one is fed with food convenient. To one he brings milk, for he is a babe; to another, he gives strong meat, for he is a man who has had his senses exercised to discern between good and evil. The steward keeps his master's stores and sees that they are not wasted; but be takes care also to magnify his master's liberality by seeing that none of the household know any want. I have known some who pretended to be stewards of Christ who evidently did not understand the business. There was an old fable of a man who gave bones to the sheep and grass to the dogs, but neither of them did well on such fare, and some preaching seems to me just like that. The preacher assumes, in his opening prayer, that all his hearers are converted, and the whole service goes on as if everybody was a Christian. Yet, if you listen carefully, you will hear that there is an undertone implying that nobody is really saved, and that everybody is saved in imagination. Brethren, if we cannot discern between the righteous and the wicked, we shall never be as God's mouth to our hearers. If we have not a javelin for God's foes, as well as butter in a lordly dish for His friends, He will never make use of us as stewards in His house. There is much grace needed in the dispensing of our Master's goods—the rightly dividing the Word of God, and bringing out every truth in due proportion and in due season.

These are two parts of the steward's business, to protect his master's property, and to dispense it.

Besides this, he is to use his master's property for his master's benefit. The goods entrusted to him are to be put out to interest or used in business to bring in profit for his master. I trust that there are many of us here present who are using the gospel for the glory of Christ. What little we know, we try to tell out that sinners may be converted and that the Savior may be glorified. It is a wonderful thing for us to have the Bible, is it not? But oh, to use the Bible every day so as to bring glory to God! It is a good thing to be even a tract-distributor or to do the least service in the kingdom of Christ. But the one point for us to aim at is to do it so that the profit of it may come, not to us, but to our Master. The steward must not get trading on his own account. As I have said before, if he does that, there is apt to be a lot of mistakes made in the reckoning; but everything that the steward does is for his master. Abraham said, "The steward of my house is this Eliezer of Damascus" (Gen. 15:2), and Abraham trusted him to go and find a wife for Isaac. So does our Lord use us and trust us as His stewards. Our great God trusts us to go and find a spouse for Christ, and our business is to go and discover her, to find her out, and ask her to come with us that she may be joined to that blessed Lord of all, the Son of the great Father, to whom He has left the inheritance. Happy are we when, like the steward of Abraham, we can bring back the beloved one for our Master's Son. This is a part of our work, to make use of everything that the Master entrusts to us for His own dear Son, and to look upon the church with which we have to deal as the bride we are to bring to Jesus that she may be married to Him forever.

I will say no more upon the first part of my subject except this: *a steward is charged with the general care of the family.* He has not merely to look after the stores, but he has to take care of all the family. The steward of the olden times used to reckon all that belonged to his master as if it were his own, and he got into the habit of talking of it in that way. His lordship once asked his steward, "What is that coming up the drive? " Oh!" he answered "it is our horse and carriage, my lord." "Our horse and carriage?" exclaimed the nobleman. "And who may be in it?" "Oh, my lord," replied the faithful servant, "it is our wife and children!" Exactly so, the man had come to look upon everything that belonged to his master as belonging to himself, and that is the spirit which our Lord would have us cultivate. Those children of His, they are our children. Those that are newly converted to God, oh, they are specially ours, mind we love them dearly! And this great church, well, it is a bride to us even as it is to Christ. Our whole self is given up to the blessed service to which Christ has given up Himself. Oh, that we could come anywhere near to this ideal of what a true steward should be! God help us so to do!

How Are We As Stewards to Behave?

Our second inquiry is, how are we who are stewards to behave?" Our text supplies the answer: "Moreover it is required in stewards, that a man be found faithful."

Note, the apostle does not say, "It is required in stewards, that a man be found brilliant." No minister will be blamed if he does not prove to be brilliant, nor even if he should not be successful. We shall not be condemned even if the seed does not spring up provided that we sow it. You are responsible not for the result of what you do but for doing it honestly, sincerely, devoutly, prayerfully, believingly. I do not think that in such a case you will be unsuccessful, certainly not as God judges success. Still, the apostle's point is that "it is required in stewards, that a man be found faithful." What, then, should each one of us be with regard to faithfulness?

First, *faithful to our Master.* Oh, whatever we do, let us not be traitors to Him! Let us not be apparently doing His work, yet not really doing it. Let us not be preaching without praying, let us not be talking about doing good without always trusting in Him without whom nothing can be good or strong or right. O God, may we each of us be able to say at the last, "I am clear of the blood of all men!" If we have dealt truly with our Master, if we can feel that we are sincerely seeking not our own glory but His glory, and working not for men but for Him alone, it is well with us.

Next, we must each one be *faithful to our office,* whatever that office may be. If you as stewards of Christ are called to be ministers, be faithful to your ministry. If you are called to have substance and to give it away, give it with cheerfulness and be faithful in your office. If you are called to teach half-a-dozen children, and no more, it is quite enough to give an account for at the last, so be faithful to your office. Do not run about finding fault with your fellow servants and thinking that you could do their work better if you had it to do. But oh, for Christ's sake, and for the sake of His great grace, do what you have to do with all your heart, mind, soul, and strength. Make full proof of your ministry, whatever that ministry is.

Then, next, be *faithful to the goods committed to you.* I have already dwelt upon the necessity of earnestly defending the faith. Oh, do not, I pray you, tolerate in yourselves any caviling at God's Word, any picking and choosing out of the great truths of inspiration! Endeavor to know the Lord's way, the Lord's truth, and the Lord's life; and in way, truth, and life, follow the Lamb wherever He goes. Search the Scriptures and follow where the Scriptures lead you. Let no book composed by the wisest of men dictate to your conscience. Remember that the Bible, and the Bible alone, has the stamp of infallibility upon it. Follow its guidance and so be faithful to the treasure that is entrusted to your hands. Had good men in past ages been but faithful to the Word of the Lord, there would not have been so much schism, heresy, and false doctrine in the world. If all professing Christians shall ever be faithful to the pure Word of God, then will come the days of the true unity of the church of Christ and the conquest of the world by Christ.

Next, we are bound to be *faithful to every person in the household.* This is a difficult work, but let us try to accomplish it. All of us, according as we are put into the stewardship, must labor for the good of all our brothers and sisters in Christ. We sang just now,

> Hast thou a lamb in all thy flock
> I would disdain to feed?

I hope that our answer is, "No, great Shepherd of Israel, there is not a single lamb in all Your flock that we do not reckon to be better than ourselves." Do you not sometimes feel as if, if you could be as sure of being right as the very least of the Lord's family, you would be perfectly content? We long to rise to the greatest heights of holiness and consecration. But, yet, if we are allowed to wash the saints' feet it would be a great honor for us. To do anything for Jesus, even be a doormat at the temple gate, is a high privilege for any one of us. Let us try, then, to do all that we ought to do in love and kindness to all the members of our Master's household.

And then we must be *faithful to the outside world* as well. You see, a steward who looked to everything indoors and then allowed people out of doors to cheat his master and run away with his goods would not be a faithful steward. You and I have much to do with the souls of men outside the church of Christ. Oh, what a world this is! What a world it is! Shall we be clear of the blood of all these millions in London? Ride or walk from one end of this great city to another and see if you do not feel a mountain of granite pressing on your soul! O Lord, what can we do? "Who is sufficient for these things?" Living in such an age as this, and in such a thronged city as this, oh, how shall we be faithful to all the people? When George Fox was dying he said, "I am clear, I am clear." I have envied him a thousand times, for I believe the Quaker was clear of the blood of men. He said many odd things, and some things he had better not have said, but he never kept back anything that seemed to come from his soul. It mattered not to whom he spoke–whether it was to the king or to a beggar–he said what he believed, without fear of mortal man. Think of brave John Knox, of whom they could say when they buried him, "Here lies he who never feared the face of man." O stewards of God–and I have already said that all of you Christians are, in your measure, stewards of Christ–may this be said of you! "It is required in stewards, that a man be found faithful." I have shown you what a wide field that one requirement covers. Only the grace of God can be sufficient for us that we may be found faithful.

How Are We in Danger of Misbehaving?

Now, very briefly indeed, I want to answer the third question, How are we, in our stewardship, in danger of misbehaving? Well, we can very readily misbehave *by acting as if we were masters.* You know the tendency of Jack in office; let us avoid anything like that. Remember what our Lord said about the man who began to domineer over his fellow servants and beat them. This is not the way for a steward to behave, for he is himself only a servant. He has to look after other servants, but his master will look after him. If he gives himself great airs, he must beware lest his master should dismiss him from his service and say to him, "Thou shalt be no longer steward."

Next, a great deal of misbehavior is caused *by endeavoring to please* men. If the steward begins to try to please his fellow servants and to curry favor with them that they may speak well of him, he will very soon be a traitor to his master. O dear friends, seek to please men for their good to edification, but never forget that he who is the servant of men cannot be the servant of God, for "no man can serve two masters" (Matt. 6:24). May the Lord help us to feel that we are not judged of men's judgment, but that we are going to do our duty as under the great Taskmaster's own eye!

Next, we can very much injure our stewardship *by idling, trifling, growing careless, or leaving our hearts out of our work.* We can do this in the Sunday school, and we can do this in the pulpit. When a man's heart is in his service, he does not need to tell you that it is, for you can soon see it; and I believe that there is more power in downright sincerity than in all the talent that God ever gave to men. A simple, humble, lowly speaker, who only says what the Holy Spirit prompts him to say, and who is quite indifferent about how he says it so long as he can say it in a right spirit, he is the man who will reach the hearts of other men. Brothers, if we begin turning over our words, so as to find out comely syllables with which we may please and tickle human ears, we shall lose all power over our hearers. I think that the very best bunch of flowers we can ever give to our friends may be made by plucking a handful of field flowers just as we find them, and then saying, "These grew in God's garden. We have not arranged them very prettily, for their innate beauty is such that anything artificial would but injure them."

Oh, let us see to it that we live wholly and alone for this great work of winning souls and glorifying our Master, and let us ever speak with the accent of conviction! If you do not believe the gospel, do not tell it to others; but if you do believe it, say it as if you meant it. I read the other day the story of a minister whose boys came to him and asked if they might go to a certain show, and he said, "Well, my dear boys, I . . . I . . . I . . . I hardly like it; I will show you by-and-by the objections there are to it. I do not decidedly forbid you." And the boys were out of the room in a minute. They ran off to their companion and said, "Jack, we may go." Yes, their father's hesitation was quite enough for them. He was going to say, "I do not decidedly forbid you, but . . . but . . . but . . ."—only the boys did not care about his "but." So, there are some ministers who in preaching say that a false doctrine is true to some extent, only there are certain objections, difficulties, and so on. People do not wait to hear the objections and difficulties, but off they go at once with a bit of bad doctrine. It is often so, and it is a pity that it should be so. Ah, me! this trifling with divine truth, this playing with God's Word, will be sure to do an infinite deal of mischief and mar the stewardship of any man who yields to it!

Next, we can prove ourselves unfaithful stewards *by misusing our Master's goods,* employing what He entrusted to us for some other end than His glory or *by neglecting some of the household.* We may so preach that there is never any milk for babes and, on the ether hand, we may so preach that there is never a morsel of meat for men, and the milk may be so watery that it is not even good enough for babes. It is a sin to neglect any one member of the household, for we must be found faithful to them all if we would be judged to be faithful at all.

We can also misbehave ourselves as stewards *by conniving at whatever is wrong in our fellow servants.* "Anything for a peaceful life!" is the motto of the unfaithful steward. "Let men live as they like. We cannot rebuke them, because then they might quarrel with us." Ah, dear me, if we are not prepared to bear a little of that sort of reproach! Even if reproof of sin must bring unkindness in return, we must not withhold that reproof, but must administer it with all the more prayerfulness and kindness. It must be given lest, as it was with Eli, a curse shall come upon our house because our sons made themselves vile, and we restrained them not.

And, dear friends, there is one other thing that any steward may do, and thereby spoil his stewardship. That is, prove unfaithful *by forgetting that his Lord will soon come.* He may come before we begin our next piece of work, He may come while we are in the middle of it, or He may come just as we are closing it and may there and then require an account at our hands. Oh, how earnestly we should live if we were sure that Christ would come tonight! What family prayer you would have tonight if you knew that before the morning dawned Christ would come! Some of you, perhaps, would want to give something extra to His cause if you knew that it would be the last opportunity you would have of doing so. Some of you would go and wake your children up and talk to them about Christ if you knew that He would come before the morning light. There is a great deal left undone by most of us. We are not all like Mr. Whitefield who could say when he went to bed, "I have not left even a pair of gloves out of their place. If I were to die tonight, everything is right." It is a beautiful thing so to live, and that is how God's stewards should live. "Ready, aye, ready," to live or to die, to go on or to leave off, to stop here or to go to heaven, just whichever the Master appoints. This is good stewardship. But if we forget that He will come, we shall get into a loose and slovenly way of acting, and that will be to our own discredit and to our Master's dishonor.

What Will Be the Result of Our Stewardship?

Now, finally, what will be the result of our stewardship? Supposing we are good stewards, what will the result be? *A reward from our Master's own lips.* In the day of account He will say, "Well done, good and faithful servant" (Matt. 25:23). Now, after that, you do not want a crown, do you? You do not want any ruling over many cities You will have all that. But I think that this utterance of our Master is quite enough for any steward of His, "Well done, good and faithful servant." Oh, if He should ever say that to us, there is enough in it to make for us a whole eternity of bliss!

But suppose that, at the last, we are found unfaithful, what will the result be? *Punishment from the Lord's own hand.* If it be so that we have never washed our robes and made them white in the blood of the Lamb; if it be so that our hearts have never been renewed by divine grace; if it be so that we have never been saved from our sin and, consequently, have never been saved from our unfaithfulness; if it should turn out that we have never been saved from living to ourselves, never been so saved as to live honestly and faithfully to God, then what will the result be? I mean, for you who profess to be Christians? Here are our Lord's words. I am not going to enlarge on them any more than I did on the other words: "The lord of that servant will come in a day when he looketh not for him, and at an hour when he is not aware, and will cut him in sunder, and will appoint him his portion with the unbelievers" (Luke 12:46)–as if that was the worst punishment that could be meted out to him. God grant that none of us may ever have that portion!

But oh, you who are unbelievers, do you not see that your portion is that which God will appoint to those who are unfaithful and only worthy of condemnation? What is your portion? It is something truly terrible, for it will be that which God appoints as a punishment for the worst of sinners, the treacherous and the unfaithful. O unbelievers, I would not be in your place five minutes for all the world! As the Lord lives, there is but a step between you and hell! Only a breath and you may be gone. If I were in your place, I should be afraid to eat a morsel of bread tonight, lest a crumb should go the wrong way, and by causing my death should land me in everlasting misery. One might be afraid to shut his eyes tonight as an unbeliever lest, as he closed them on earth, he shut them forever to all light and hope, world without end.

> Ye sinners, seek his grace,
>   Whose wrath ye cannot bear;
> Fly to the shelter of his cross,
>   And find salvation there.

Oh, fly to Jesus at once, for He has said, "Him that cometh to me I will in no wise cast out" (John 6:37). God help you to trust to Christ tonight and to go out of this Tabernacle saved men and saved women, for Jesus Christ's sake! Amen.